The Biggest Ever
Knock Knock
Joke Book

The Biggest Ever Knock Knock Joke Book

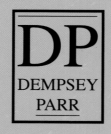

DP

DEMPSEY
PARR

This is a Dempsey Parr Book
First published in 2000

Dempsey Parr is an imprint of Parragon
Parragon
Queen Street House
4 Queen Street
Bath
BA1 1HE, UK

Produced by Magpie Books, an imprint of
Constable & Robinson Ltd, London

Copyright © Parragon 2000

ISBN 1-84084-955-X

A copy of the British Library Cataloguing-in-Publication Data
is available from the British Library

Printed and bound in Indonesia

10 9 8 7 6 5 4 3 2 1

Introduction

Knock knock, who's there? Albert you'll never guess! Is it Pierre through the keyhole or Hayden behind the door? But wait a minute, Donovan that door – it could be Jimmy all your money or Eva had a smack in the mouth! Better look through the spyhole first, Justine case – oh good, it's only Edna cloud and her friend, Fayeding away. But who will it be next time? They're all here, hundreds of them, just waiting to knock at YOUR door, right now!

Knock knock.
Who's there?
Aaron.
Aaron who?
Aaron on the chest means strength
   in the arms.

Knock knock.
Who's there?
Aaron.
Aaron who?
Aaron'd boy, of course!

Knock knock.
Who's there?
Abba.
Abba who?
Abba'out turn!
Quick march!

Knock knock.
Who's there?
Abel.
Abel who?
Abel to see you, ha, ha!

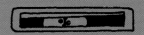

Knock knock.
Who's there?
Abel.
Abel who?
Abel to go to work.

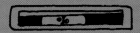

Knock knock.
Who's there?
Adair.
Adair who?
Adair you to open this door.

Knock knock.
Who's there?
Adam.
Adam who?
Adam will burst any minute now.

Knock knock.
Who's there?
Adam.
Adam who?
Adam nuisance come to borrow
   some sugar.

Knock knock.
Who's there?
Abyssinia.
Abyssinia who?
Abyssinia next term!

Knock knock.
Who's there?
Ada.
Ada who?
Ada lot for breakfast.

Knock knock.
Who's there?
Adder.
Adder who?
Adder you get in here?

Knock knock.
Who's there?
Ahab.
Ahab who?
Ahab to go to the bathroom in a
	hurry, open the door quick!

Knock knock.
Who's there?
Ahmed.
Ahmed who?
Ahmed a big mistake coming here!

Knock knock.
Who's there?
Aida.
Aida who?
Aida whole box of chocolates and I
	feel really sick.

Knock knock.
Who's there?
Aida.
Aida who?
Aida whole village cos I'm a
	monster.

Knock knock.
Who's there?
Aileen.
Aileen who?
Aileen against my Rolls-Royce.

Knock knock.
Who's there?
Aitch.
Aitch who?
Bless you.

Knock knock.
Who's there?
Al.
Al who?
Al be seeing you!

Knock knock.
Who's there?
Alan.
Alan who?
Alan a good cause.

Knock knock.
Who's there?
Alaska.
Alaska who?
Alaska one more time.

Knock knock.
Who's there?
Alaska.
Alaska who?
Alaska the teacher if I can leave the room.

Knock knock.
Who's there?
Albert.
Albert who?
Albert you'll never guess.

Knock knock.
Who's there?
Aldo.
Aldo who?
Aldo the washing-up tonight.

Knock knock.
Who's there?
Alec.
Alec who?
Alec your sister but I don't like you.

Knock knock.
Who's there?
Aleta.
Aleta who?
Aleta bit of lovin'.

Knock knock.
Who's there?
Alexander.
Alexander who?
Alexander friend want to come over.

Knock knock.
Who's there?
Alf.
Alf who?
Alf all if you don't catch me!

Knock knock.
Who's there?
Aleta.
Aleta who?
Aleta from your bank manager.

Knock knock.
Who's there?
Alf.
Alf who?
Alf way home.

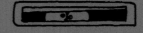

Knock knock.
Who's there?
Alex.
Alex who?
Alex plain later if you let me in.

Knock knock.
Who's there?
Alfie.
Alfie who?
Alfie terrible if you leave.

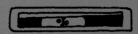

Knock knock.
Who's there?
Ali.
Ali who?
Ali cat.

Knock knock.
Who's there?
Alice.
Alice who?
Alice on your new house.

Knock knock.
Who's there?
Alison.
Alison who?
Alison to my teacher.

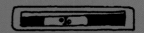

Knock knock.
Who's there?
Alison.
Alison who?
Alison Wonderland.

Knock knock.
Who's there?
Alistair.
Alistair who?
Alistairs in this house are broken.

Knock knock.
Who's there?
Alma.
Alma who?
Almany times do I have to knock?

Knock knock.
Who's there?
Alma.
Alma who?
Alma lovin'.

Knock knock.
Who's there?
Alma.
Alma who?
Alma not going to tell you!

Knock knock.
Who's there?
Almond.
Almond who?
Almond come in, I'm expected here.

Knock knock.
Who's there?
Althea.
Althea who?
Althea in court.

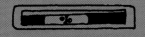

Knock knock.
Who's there?
Alvin.
Alvin who?
Alvin zis competition – just vait and
    see!

Knock knock.
Who's there?
Amanda.
Amanda who?
Amanda the table.

Knock knock.
Who's there?
Amber.
Amber who?
Amberter than I was yesterday.

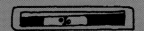

Knock knock.
Who's there?
Amber.
Amber who?
Amber-sting to go to the bathroom!

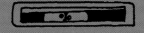

Knock knock.
Who's there?
Amin.
Amin who?
Amin man.

Knock knock.
Who's there?
Ammonia.
Ammonia who?
Ammonia poor boy, nobody loves me.

Knock knock.
Who's there?
Amos.
Amos who?
Amosquito.

Knock knock.
Who's there?
Amos.
Amos who?
Amos be mad! This isn't my house!

Knock knock.
Who's there?
Amy.
Amy who?
Amy for the top.

Knock knock.
Who's there?
Anais.
Anais who?
Anais cup of tea.

Knock knock.
Who's there?
Andrew.
Andrew who?
Andrew a picture on the wall.

Knock knock.
Who's there?
Andy.
Andy who?
Andy man.

Knock knock.
Who's there?
Anita Loos.
Anita Loos who?
Anita Loos about 20 pounds.

Knock knock.
Who's there?
Ann.
Ann who?
Ann amazingly good joke.

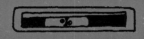

Knock knock.
Who's there?
Annette.
Annette who?
Annette curtain looks good in the
    window.

Knock knock.
Who's there?
Annie.
Annie who?
Annie one you like.

Knock knock.
Who's there?
Anna.
Anna who?
Annather mosquito.

Knock knock.
Who's there?
Annabel.
Annabel who?
Annabel would be useful on this
    door.

Knock knock.
Who's there?
Anya.
Anya who?
Anya best behavior.

Knock knock.
Who's there?
Apple.
Apple who?
Apple the door myself.

Knock knock.
Who's there?
April.
April who?
April will make you feel better.

Knock knock.
Who's there?
Argo.
Argo who?
Argo to piano lessons after school.

Knock knock.
Who's there?
Armageddon.
Armageddon who?
Armageddon out of here quick.

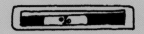

Knock knock.
Who's there?
Army Ant.
Army Ant who?
Army Ants coming for tea then?

Knock knock.
Who's there?
Arnie.
Arnie who?
Arnie going to let me in?

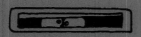

Knock knock.
Who's there?
Arnold.
Arnold who?
Arnold man.

Knock knock.
Who's there?
Asa.
Asa who?
Asa glass of orange out of the
    question?

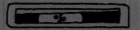

Knock knock.
Who's there?
Asia.
Asia who?
Asia mom in?

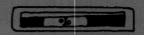

Knock knock.
Who's there?
Athens.
Athens who?
Athenshadow over the moon.

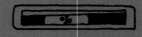

Knock knock.
Who's there?
Atomic.
Atomic who?
Atomic ache is hard to stomach.

Knock knock.
Who's there?
Attila.
Attila who?
Attila you no lies.

Knock knock.
Who's there?
Audrey.
Audrey who?
Audrey to pay for this?

Knock knock.
Who's there?
Audrey.
Audrey who?
Audrey lots of water.

Knock knock.
Who's there?
Augusta.
Augusta who?
Augusta wind will blow the witch
    away.

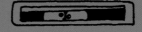

Knock knock.
Who's there?
Augusta.
Augusta who?
Augustalmost felt like winter.

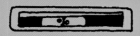

Knock knock.
Who's there?
Auntie.
Auntie who?
Auntie glad to see me again?

Knock knock.
Who's there?
Aurora.
Aurora who?
Aurora's just come from a big lion!

Knock knock.
Who's there?
Austen.
Austen who?
Austentatiously rich.

Knock knock.
Who's there?
Ava.
Ava who?
Ava good mind to leave you.

Knock knock.
Who's there?
Avenue.
Avenue who?
Avenue learned my name yet?

Knock knock.
Who's there?
Avis.
Avis who?
Avisibly shaken person.

Knock knock.
Who's there?
Baby.
Baby who?
(sing) "Baby love, my baby love . . ."

Knock knock.
Who's there?
Baby Owl.
Baby Owl who?
Baby Owl see you later, baby not.

Knock knock.
Who's there?
Bach.
Bach who?
Bach to work.

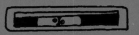

Knock knock.
Who's there?
Bacon.
Bacon who?
Bacon a cake in the oven.

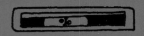

Knock knock.
Who's there?
Barbara.
Barbara who?
(sing) "Barbara black sheep, have
    you any wool?"

Knock knock.
Who's there?
Barbie.
Barbie who?
Barbie Q.

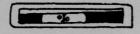

Knock knock.
Who's there?
Bark.
Bark who?
Bark your car in the garage.

Knock knock.
Who's there?
Barry.
Barry who?
Barry the dead.

Knock knock.
Who's there?
Basket.
Basket who?
Basket home, it's nearly dark.

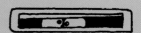

Knock knock.
Who's there?
Bass.
Bass who?
Basstion of the law.

Knock knock.
Who's there?
Bat.
Bat who?
Bat you'll never guess!

Knock knock.
Who's there?
Bea.
Bea who?
Bea love and open the door.

Knock knock.
Who's there?
Bean.
Bean who?
Bean anywhere nice for your
    vacation?

Knock knock.
Who's there?
Becca.
Becca who?
Becca the net.

Knock knock.
Who's there?
Becker.
Becker who?
Becker the devil you know.

Knock knock.
Who's there?
Bed.
Bed who?
Bed you can't guess who it is!

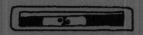

Knock knock.
Who's there?
Bee.
Bee who?
Bee careful out there!

Knock knock.
Who's there?
Beef.
Beef who?
Beef fair!

Knock knock.
Who's there?
Belize.
Belize who?
Oh, Belize yourself then.

Knock knock.
Who's there?
Bella.
Bella who?
Bella the ball.

Knock knock.
Who's there?
Belle.
Belle who?
Belle-t up and open the door.

Knock knock.
Who's there?
Ben.
Ben who?
Ben down and tie your shoelaces.

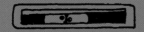

Knock knock.
Who's there?
Ben and Anna.
Ben and Anna who?
Ben and Anna split.

Knock knock.
Who's there?
Ben Hur.
Ben Hur who?
Ben Hur an hour – let me in!

Knock knock.
Who's there?
Benin.
Benin who?
Benin hell.

Knock knock.
Who's there?
Benin.
Benin who?
Benin in a good mood lately.

Knock knock.
Who's there?
Benjamin.
Benjamin who?
Benjamin the blues.

Knock knock.
Who's there?
Berlin.
Berlin who?
Berlin maiden over.

Knock knock.
Who's there?
Bernadette.
Bernadette who?
Bernadette my dinner.

Knock knock.
Who's there?
Bernie.
Bernie who?
Bernie bridges.

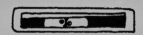

Knock knock.
Who's there?
Bert.
Bert who?
Bert the cakes.

Knock knock.
Who's there?
Bertha.
Bertha who?
Bertha day boy.

Knock knock.
Who's there?
Beth.
Beth who?
Beth foot forward.

Knock knock.
Who's there?
Bethany.
Bethany who?
Bethany good shows recently?

Knock knock.
Who's there?
Bette.
Bette who?
Bette of roses.

Knock knock.
Who's there?
Bettina.
Bettina who?
Bettina minute you'll go to sleep.

Knock knock.
Who's there?
Betty.
Betty who?
Betty earns a lot of money.

Knock knock.
Who's there?
Bhuto.
Bhuto who?
Bhuton the other foot.

Knock knock.
Who's there?
Bill.
Bill who?
Bill of rights.

Knock knock.
Who's there?
Billy Bragg.
Billy Bragg who?
Billy Braggs too much – tell him to
   stop.

Knock knock.
Who's there?
Biro.
Biro who?
Biro light of the moon.

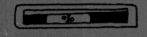

Knock knock.
Who's there?
Bjorn.
Bjorn who?
Bjorn in the USA.

Knock knock.
Who's there?
Bjorn.
Bjorn who?
Bjorn free.

Knock knock.
Who's there?
Blair.
Blair who?
Blair play.

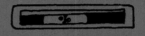

Knock knock.
Who's there?
Blanche.
Blanche who?
Blanche not.

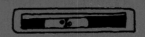

Knock knock.
Who's there?
Blood.
Blood who?
Blood brothers.

Knock knock.
Who's there?
Blue.
Blue who?
Blue away with the wind.

Knock knock.
Who's there?
Blur.
Blur who?
Blur! It's cold out here.

Knock knock.
Who's there?
Bobby.
Bobby who?
Bobbyn up and down like this.

Knock knock.
Who's there?
Bolton.
Bolton who?
Bolton braces.

Knock knock.
Who's there?
Bones.
Bones who?
Bones upon a time . . .

Knock knock.
Who's there?
Boo.
Boo who?
Oh please don't cry!

Knock knock.
Who's there?
Borg.
Borg who?
Borg standard.

Knock knock.
Who's there?
Bosnia.
Bosnia who?
Bosnia bell here earlier?

Knock knock.
Who's there?
Bowl.
Bowl who?
Bowl me over.

Knock knock.
Who's there?
Boyzone.
Boyzone who?
Boyzone adventures.

Knock knock.
Who's there?
Brad.
Brad who?
Brad to meet ya!

Knock knock.
Who's there?
Brazil.
Brazil who?
Brazil hold your breasts up.

Knock knock.
Who's there?
Brendan.
Brendan who?
Brendan an ear to what I have to
    say.

Knock knock.
Who's there?
Brian.
Brian who?
Brian drain!

Knock knock.
Who's there?
Bridget.
Bridget who?
Bridget the end of the world.

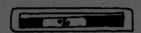

Knock knock.
Who's there?
Bridie.
Bridie who?
Bridie light of the silvery moon.

Knock knock.
Who's there?
Brighton.
Brighton who?
Brightonder the light of the full
    moon.

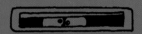

Knock knock.
Who's there?
Briony.
Briony who?
Briony, beautiful sea.

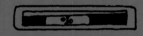

Knock knock.
Who's there?
Bronte.
Bronte who?
Bronte of the blow.

Knock knock.
Who's there?
Bruno.
Bruno who?
Bruno more tea for me.

Knock knock.
Who's there?
Bug.
Bug who?
Bug Rogers.

Knock knock.
Who's there?
Brook.
Brook who?
Brooklyn Bridge.

Knock knock.
Who's there?
Brother.
Brother who?
Brotheration! I've forgotten my own
    name!

Knock knock.
Who's there?
Bug.
Bug who?
Bugsy Malone.

Knock knock.
Who's there?
Bull.
Bull who?
Bull the chain.

Knock knock.
Who's there?
Bun.
Bun who?
Bunnies make the best pets.

Knock knock.
Who's there?
Burglar.
Burglar who?
Burglars don't knock.

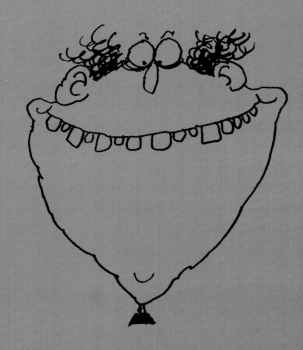

Knock knock.
Who's there?
Buster.
Buster who?
Buster blood vessel.

Knock knock.
Who's there?
Buster.
Buster who?
Buster the town, please.

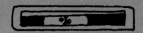

Knock knock.
Who's there?
Butcher.
Butcher who?
Butcher left leg in, your left leg
    out . . .

Knock knock.
Who's there?
Butter.
Butter who?
Butter wrap up – it's cold out here.

Knock knock.
Who's there?
Butter.
Butter who?
Butter hurry up – I need the toilet
    now!

Knock knock.
Who's there?
Byron.
Byron who?
Byron new suit.

Knock knock.
Who's there?
Caesar.
Caesar who?
Caesar arm to stop her getting
 away.

Knock knock.
Who's there?
Caesar.
Caesar who?
Caesar jolly good fellow.

Knock knock.
Who's there?
Cain.
Cain who?
Cain tell you.

Knock knock.
Who's there?
Caitlin.
Caitlin who?
Caitlin you my dress tonight – I'm
 wearing it.

Knock knock.
Who's there?
Callum.
Callum who?
Callum all back.

Knock knock.
Who's there?
Camilla.
Camilla who?
Camilla minute.

Knock knock.
Who's there?
Candace.
Candace who?
Candace be love?

Knock knock.
Who's there?
Canoe.
Canoe who?
Canoe lend me some money?

Knock knock.
Who's there?
Canon.
Canon who?
Canon open the door then.

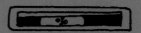

Knock knock.
Who's there?
Card.
Card who?
Card you see it's me!

Knock knock.
Who's there?
Carl.
Carl who?
Carl you see?

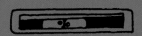

Knock knock.
Who's there?
Carlene.
Carlene who?
Carlene against that wall!

Knock knock.
Who's there?
Carlo.
Carlo who?
Carload of junk.

Knock knock.
Who's there?
Carmen.
Carmen who?
Carmen like best is a Ferrari.

Knock knock.
Who's there?
Carol.
Carol who?
Carol go if you switch the ignition
    on.

Knock knock.
Who's there?
Caroline.
Caroline who?
Caroline of rope with you.

Knock knock.
Who's there?
Carrie.
Carrie who?
Carrie on with what you were doing.

Knock knock.
Who's there?
Cassie.
Cassie who?
Cassie you some time?

Knock knock.
Who's there?
Cat.
Cat who?
Cat you understand?

Knock knock.
Who's there?
Caterpillar.
Caterpillar who?
Caterpillar a few mice for you.

Knock knock.
Who's there?
Cattle.
Cattle who?
Cattle purr if you stroke it.

Knock knock.
Who's there?
Cecile.
Cecile who?
Cecile th-the w-windows. Th-there's
    a m-monster out there.

Knock knock.
Who's there?
Cecile.
Cecile who?
Cecile the envelope.

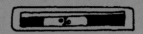

Knock knock.
Who's there?
Celeste.
Celeste who?
Celeste time I come calling.

Knock knock.
Who's there?
Cello.
Cello who?
Cello, how are you?

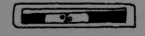

Knock knock.
Who's there?
Chad.
Chad who?
Chad you could come.

Knock knock.
Who's there?
Chapman.
Chapman who?
Chapmany times if you like the
  show.

Knock knock.
Who's there?
Charles.
Charles who?
Charles your luck on the roulette
  wheel.

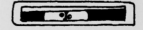

Knock knock.
Who's there?
Census.
Census who?
Census presents for Christmas.

Knock knock.
Who's there?
Cereal.
Cereal who?
Cereal pleasure to meet you.

Knock knock.
Who's there?
Che.
Che who?
Che what you're made of.

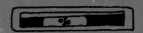

Knock knock.
Who's there?
Cheese.
Cheese who?
Cheese a jolly good fellow.

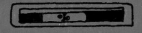

Knock knock.
Who's there?
Cher.
Cher who?
Cher and share alike!

Knock knock.
Who's there?
Chest.
Chest who?
Chestnuts for sale!

Knock knock.
Who's there?
Chester.
Chester who?
Chester drawers.

Knock knock.
Who's there?
Chester.
Chester who?
Chester minute! Don't you know who
    I am?

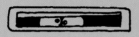

Knock knock.
Who's there?
Chicken.
Chicken who?
Chicken your pockets – I think your
    keys are there.

Knock knock.
Who's there?
Chile.
Chile who?
Chile without your coat on!

Knock knock.
Who's there?
Chin and Tony.
Chin and Tony who?
Chin and Tonyk.

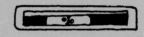

Knock knock.
Who's there?
Choc-ice.
Choc-ice who?
Choc-ice into this glass, would you?

Knock knock.
Who's there?
Chris.
Chris who?
Christmas stocking.

Knock knock.
Who's there?
Chrome.
Chrome who?
Chromosome.

Knock knock.
Who's there?
Chocs.
Chocs who?
Chocs away!

Knock knock.
Who's there?
Chopin.
Chopin who?
Chopin the department store.

Knock knock.
Who's there?
Chrysalis.
Chrysalis who?
Chrysalis the cake for you.

Knock knock.
Who's there?
Chuck.
Chuck who?
Chuck in a sandwich for lunch!

Knock knock.
Who's there?
Churchill.
Churchill who?
Churchill be the best place for your
   wedding.

Knock knock.
Who's there?
Cindy.
Cindy who?
Cindy parcel special delivery.

Knock knock.
Who's there?
Clara.
Clara who?
Clara space on the table.

Knock knock.
Who's there?
Clarence.
Clarence who?
Clarence Sale.

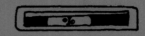

Knock knock.
Who's there?
Clark.
Clark who?
Clark your car out here.

Knock knock.
Who's there?
Claudette.
Claudette who?
Claudette a whole cake.

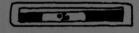

Knock knock.
Who's there?
Clay.
Clay who?
Clay on, Sam.

Knock knock.
Who's there?
Cliff.
Cliff who?
Cliff hanger.

Knock knock.
Who's there?
Clinton.
Clinton who?
Clinton your eye.

Knock knock.
Who's there?
Closure.
Closure who?
Closure mouth when you're eating!

Knock knock.
Who's there?
Coffin.
Coffin who?
Coffin and spluttering.

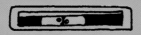

Knock knock.
Who's there?
Cohen.
Cohen who?
Cohen your way.

Knock knock.
Who's there?
Cole.
Cole who?
Cole as a cucumber.

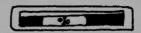

Knock knock.
Who's there?
Colin.
Colin who?
Colin and see me next time you're
     passing.

Knock knock.
Who's there?
Colin.
Colin who?
Colin all cars . . . Colin all cars . . .

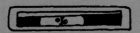

Knock knock.
Who's there?
Colleen.
Colleen who?
Colleen yourself up, you're a mess!

Knock knock.
Who's there?
Collie.
Collie who?
Collie Miss Molly, I don't know.

Knock knock.
Who's there?
Cologne.
Cologne who?
Cologne around the world and meet
   people.

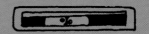

Knock knock.
Who's there?
Congo.
Congo who?
Congo into the woods – it's
   dangerous.

Knock knock.
Who's there?
Congo.
Congo who?
We congo on meeting behind the
    bookshelves.

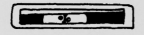

Knock knock.
Who's there?
Cook.
Cook who?
Cuckoo yourself! I didn't come here
    to be insulted.

Knock knock.
Who's there?
Cookie.
Cookie who?
Cookien the kitchen – it's easier.

Knock knock.
Who's there?
Corrinne.
Corrinne who?
Corrinne the bell now.

Knock knock.
Who's there?
Cosmo.
Cosmo who?
Cosmo trouble than you're worth!

Knock knock.
Who's there?
Costas.
Costas who?
Costas a fortune to get here.

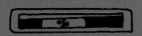

Knock knock.
Who's there?
Courtney.
Courtney who?
Courtney robbers lately?

Knock knock.
Who's there?
Courtney Pine.
Courtney Pine who?
Courtney Pine tables? I want to buy one.

Knock knock.
Who's there?
Cousin.
Cousin who?
Cousin stead of opening the door you're leaving me here.

Knock knock.
Who's there?
Craig.
Craig who?
Craig in the wall.

Knock knock.
Who's there?
Cream.
Cream who?
Cream louder so the police will
    come.

Knock knock.
Who's there?
Crete.
Crete who?
Crete to see you.

Knock knock.
Who's there?
Crete.
Crete who?
Crete to be safe at last.

Knock knock.
Who's there?
Cricket.
Cricket who?
Cricket neck means I can't bend
    over.

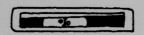

Knock knock.
Who's there?
Crispin.
Crispin who?
Crispin crunchy is how I like my
    cereal.

Knock knock.
Who's there?
Crock and Dial.
Crock and Dial who?
Crock and Dial Dundee.

Knock knock.
Who's there?
Cuba.
Cuba who?
Cuba wood.

Knock knock.
Who's there?
Curry.
Curry who?
Curry me all the way.

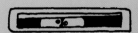

Knock knock.
Who's there?
Cynthia.
Cynthia who?
Cynthia won't listen, I'll keep
    shouting.

Knock knock.
Who's there?
Cyprus.
Cyprus who?
Cyprus the bell?

Knock knock.
Who's there?
Cyril.
Cyril who?
Cyril animals at the zoo.

Knock knock.
Who's there?
Cyril.
Cyril who?
Cyril pleasure when you leave!

Knock knock.
Who's there?
Czech.
Czech who?
Czech before you open the door!

Knock knock.
Who's there?
Dad.
Dad who?
Dadda! Let's roll out the red carpet!

Knock knock.
Who's there?
Daisy.
Daisy who?
Daisy that you are in, but I don't
    believe them.

Knock knock.
Who's there?
Dakota.
Dakota who?
Dakota is too small around the
    neck.

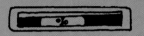

Knock knock.
Who's there?
Dale.
Dale who?
Dale come if you call dem.

Knock knock.
Who's there?
Dana.
Dana who?
Dana you mind.

Knock knock.
Who's there?
Danielle.
Danielle who?
Danielle so loud, I heard you the
    first time.

Knock knock.
Who's there?
Danny.
Danny who?
Dannybody home?

Knock knock.
Who's there?
Darren.
Darren who?
Darren the garden, hiding.

Knock knock.
Who's there?
Daryl.
Daryl who?
Daryl be the day.

Knock knock.
Who's there?
Datsun.
Datsun who?
Datsun other lousy joke!

Knock knock.
Who's there?
Dave.
Dave who?
Dave-andalized our home.

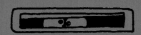

Knock knock.
Who's there?
Dave.
Dave who?
Dave of glory.

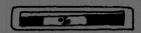

Knock knock.
Who's there?
Dawn.
Dawn who?
Dawn do anything I wouldn't do.

Knock knock.
Who's there?
Debbie.
Debbie who?
Debbie or not to be.

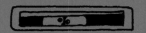

Knock knock.
Who's there?
Debussy.
Debussy who?
Debussy's never on time!

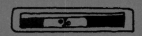

Knock knock.
Who's there?
Delhi.
Delhi who?
Delhi a joke . . .

Knock knock.
Who's there?
Della.
Della who?
Della tell ya that I love ya?

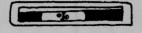

Knock knock.
Who's there?
Delphine.
Delphine who?
Delphine fine, thanks.

Knock knock.
Who's there?
Delta.
Delta who?
Delta great hand of cards.

Knock knock.
Who's there?
Demi Moore.
Demi Moore who?
Demi Moore than you did last time.

Knock knock.
Who's there?
Denise.
Denise who?
Denise are above de feet.

Knock knock.
Who's there?
Denmark.
Denmark who?
Denmark your own territory.

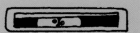

Knock knock.
Who's there?
Depp.
Depp who?
Depp inside dear!

Knock knock.
Who's there?
Denial.
Denial who?
Denial flows through Egypt.

Knock knock.
Who's there?
De Niro.
De Niro who?
De Niro you get, the faster I run.

Knock knock.
Who's there?
Derek.
Derek who?
Derek get richer and the poor get
    poorer.

Knock knock.
Who's there?
Desi.
Desi who?
Desi take sugar?

Knock knock.
Who's there?
Devlin.
Devlin who?
Devlin a red dress.

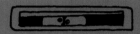

Knock knock.
Who's there?
Dewey.
Dewey who?
Dewey stay or do we go now?

Knock knock.
Who's there?
Diana.
Diana who?
Diana thirst – a glass of water,
    please.

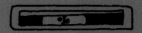

Knock knock.
Who's there?
Diaz.
Diaz who?
Diaz of our lives.

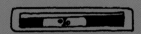

Knock knock.
Who's there?
Dickon.
Dickon who?
Dickon the right answer.

Knock knock.
Who's there?
Diego.
Diego who?
Diego before de "B."

Knock knock.
Who's there?
Diesel.
Diesel who?
Diesel make you feel better.

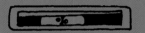

Knock knock.
Who's there?
Dimaggio.
Dimaggio who?
Dimaggio yourself on a deserted
    island . . .

Knock knock.
Who's there?
Disc.
Disc who?
Discusting!

Knock knock.
Who's there?
Dish.
Dish who?
Dish ish a shtick-up!

Knock knock.
Who's there?
Dishwasher.
Dishwasher who?
Dishwasher way I shpoke before I
had my teef fixshed.

Knock knock.
Who's there?
Dismay.
Dismay who?
Dismay surprise you but I'm from
New York.

Knock knock.
Who's there?
Distress.
Distress who?
Distress is brand new.

Knock knock.
Who's there?
Doctor.
Doctor Who?
That's right – where's my Tardis?

Knock knock.
Who's there?
Dolly.
Dolly who?
Dolly't us in, we're cold!

Knock knock.
Who's there?
Dome.
Dome who?
Dome you recognize my voice?

Knock knock.
Who's there?
Don.
Don who?
Don take me for granted.

Knock knock.
Who's there?
Donna.
Donna who?
Donna you know? Isa Luigi.

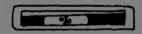

Knock knock.
Who's there?
Dorothy.
Dorothy who?
(sing) "Dorothynk I'm sexy?"

Knock knock.
Who's there?
Dot.
Dot who?
Dot to dot.

Knock knock.
Who's there?
Doughnut.
Doughnut who?
Doughnut open the door whatever
   you do.

Knock knock.
Who's there?
Donovan.
Donovan who?
Donovan the door – it's dangerous.

Knock knock.
Who's there?
Dora.
Dora who?
Dora steel.

Knock knock.
Who's there?
Douglas.
Douglas who?
Douglas is broken.

Knock knock.
Who's there?
Dozen.
Dozen who?
Dozen anyone know my name?

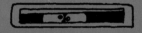

Knock knock.
Who's there?
Drum.
Drum who?
Drum as fast as you can.

Knock knock.
Who's there?
Duane.
Duane who?
Duane gonna get away with dis!

Knock knock.
Who's there?
Dublin.
Dublin who?
Dublin up with laughter.

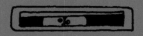

Knock knock.
Who's there?
Duke.
Duke who?
Duke come here often?

Knock knock.
Who's there?
Duncan.
Duncan who?
Duncan make your garden grow.

Knock knock.
Who's there?
Duncan.
Duncan who?
Duncan biscuit in your tea.

Knock knock.
Who's there?
Duncan.
Duncan who?
Duncan Disorderly.

Knock knock.
Who's there?
Dutch.
Dutch who?
Dutch me in the morning.

Knock knock.
Who's there?
Dwight.
Dwight who?
Dwight house is where the
    president lives.

Knock knock.
Who's there?
Eamon.
Eamon who?
Eamon a good mood – have my
    piece of cake.

Knock knock.
Who's there?
Ear.
Ear who?
Ear you are – a letter.

Knock knock.
Who's there?
Earl.
Earl who?
Earl tell you if you open the door.

Knock knock.
Who's there?
Ears.
Ears who?
Ears looking at you kid.

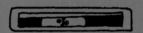

Knock knock.
Who's there?
Earwig.
Earwig who?
Earwigo!

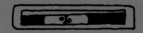

Knock knock.
Who's there?
Edna.
Edna who?
Edna way.

Knock knock.
Who's there?
Edward.
Edward who?
Edward like to play now, please.

Knock knock.
Who's there?
Edwin.
Edwin who?
Edwin a cup if I could run faster.

Knock knock.
Who's there?
Eddie.
Eddie who?
Eddie-body you like.

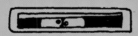

Knock knock.
Who's there?
Edna.
Edna who?
Edna cloud.

Knock knock.
Who's there?
Eel.
Eel who?
Eel meet again.

Knock knock.
Who's there?
Effie.
Effie who?
Effie'd known you were coming
   he'd have stayed home.

Knock knock.
Who's there?
Egbert.
Egbert who?
Egbert no bacon.

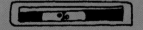

Knock knock.
Who's there?
Egg.
Egg who?
Eggsactly.

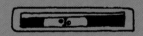

Knock knock.
Who's there?
Egypt.
Egypt who?
Egypt me out in the cold!

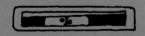

Knock knock.
Who's there?
Eileen.
Eileen who?
Eileen against the door.

Knock knock.
Who's there?
Eisenhower.
Eisenhower who?
Eisenhower late for work.

Knock knock.
Who's there?
Eli.
Eli who?
Elies all the time.

Knock knock.
Who's there?
Eli.
Eli who?
Eli, eli, oh!

Knock knock.
Who's there?
Elizabeth.
Elizabeth who?
Elizabeth of knowledge is a
    dangerous thing.

Knock knock.
Who's there?
Ella.
Ella who?
Ella've good night!

Knock knock.
Who's there?
Ellen.
Ellen who?
Ellen all the ghouls are after me.

Knock knock.
Who's there?
Ellie.
Ellie who.
Ellie Phant.

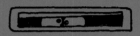

Knock knock.
Who's there?
Miss Ellie.
Miss Ellie who?
Miss Ellie good shows lately?

Knock knock.
Who's there?
Ellis.
Ellis who?
Ellis damnation.

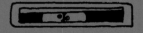

Knock knock.
Who's there?
Ellis.
Ellis who?
Ellis before "M."

Knock knock.
Who's there?
Elly.
Elly who?
Ellymentary, my dear Watson.

Knock knock.
Who's there?
Elsie.
Elsie who?
Elsie you in court!

Knock knock.
Who's there?
Elton.
Elton who?
Elton old lady to cross the road.

Knock knock.
Who's there?
Elvis.
Elvis who?
Elviseeing you some time.

Knock knock.
Who's there?
Emil.
Emil who?
Emil would be nice if you've got
    some food.

Knock knock.
Who's there?
Emma.
Emma who?
Emma new neighbor – come round
    for tea.

Knock knock.
Who's there?
Emmett.
Emmett who?
Emmett the front door, not the
    back.

Knock knock.
Who's there?
Enid.
Enid who?
Enid a glass of water.

Knock knock.
Who's there?
Enoch.
Enoch who?
Enoch and Enoch but no one
    answers the door!

Knock knock.
Who's there?
Erica.
Erica who?
Erica'd the last sweet.

Knock knock.
Who's there?
Erin.
Erin who?
Erin your lungs.

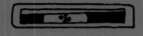

Knock knock.
Who's there?
Esau.
Esau who?
Esau you in the bath!

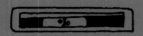

Knock knock.
Who's there?
Ethan.
Ethan who?
Ethan people don't go to church.

Knock knock.
Who's there?
Ethan.
Ethan who?
Ethan all my dinner.

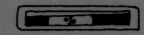

Knock knock.
Who's there?
Eugene.
Eugene who?
Eugene, me Tarzan.

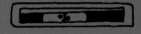

Knock knock.
Who's there?
Eunice.
Eunice who?
Eunice is like your nephew.

Knock knock.
Who's there?
Eunice.
Eunice who?
Eunice is a witch – I thought you
    should know.

Knock knock.
Who's there?
Euripides.
Euripides who?
Euripides, you pay for a new pair.

Knock knock.
Who's there?
Europe.
Europe who?
Europening the door very slowly.

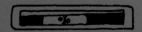

Knock knock.
Who's there?
Eva.
Eva who?
Eva had a smack in the mouth?

Knock knock.
Who's there?
Evan.
Evan who?
Evan you should know who it is.

Knock knock.
Who's there?
Evan.
Evan who?
Evan only knows!

Knock knock.
Who's there?
Eve.
Eve who?
Eve-ho, here we go.

Knock knock.
Who's there?
Evie.
Evie who?
Evie weather.

Knock knock.
Who's there?
Ewan.
Ewan who?
Ewan me should get together.

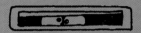

Knock knock.
Who's there?
Ewan.
Ewan who?
No one else, just me!

Knock knock.
Who's there?
Eye.
Eye who?
Eye know who you are.

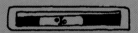

Knock knock.
Who's there?
Ezra.
Ezra who?
Ezra room to rent?

Knock knock.
Who's there?
Fang.
Fang who?
Fangs for the memory.

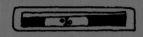

Knock knock.
Who's there?
Fang.
Fang who?
Fang you for having me.

Knock knock.
Who's there?
Fanny.
Fanny who?
Fanny you not knowing who I am!

Knock knock.
Who's there?
Fanta.
Fanta who?
Fanta Claus.

Knock knock.
Who's there?
Fantasy.
Fantasy who?
Fantasy a walk in the park?

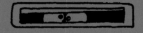

Knock knock.
Who's there?
Fax.
Fax who?
Fax you very much.

Knock knock.
Who's there?
Faye.
Faye who?
Fayeding away.

Knock knock.
Who's there?
Felicity.
Felicity who?
Felicity getting more polluted every day.

Knock knock.
Who's there?
Felipe.
Felipe who?
Felipe bath – I need a wash!

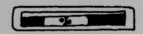

Knock knock.
Who's there?
Felix.
Felix who?
Felix his bottom again I'll scream!

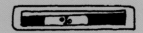

Knock knock.
Who's there?
Felix.
Felix who?
Felixtremely cold.

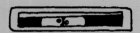

Knock knock.
Who's there?
Fergie.
Fergie who?
Fergiedness sake let me in!

Knock knock.
Who's there?
Few.
Few who?
Few! What's that smell?

Knock knock.
Who's there?
Fiddle.
Fiddle who?
Fiddle-dee-dee.

Knock knock.
Who's there?
Fido.
Fido who?
Fido known you were coming I'd have bolted all the doors.

Knock knock.
Who's there?
Fido.
Fido who?
Fido known you were coming I'd
    have baked a cake.

Knock knock.
Who's there?
Fifi.
Fifi who?
Fifiling c-cold, p-please l-let m-me
    in.

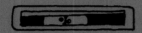

Knock knock.
Who's there?
Fig.
Fig who?
Figs the step, it's broken.

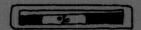

Knock knock.
Who's there?
Fiona.
Fiona who?
Fiona large house and a car.

Knock knock.
Who's there?
Fish.
Fish who?
Bless you!

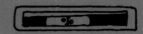

Knock knock.
Who's there?
Flea.
Flea who?
Flea's a jolly good feller!

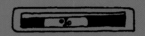

Knock knock.
Who's there?
Fitzwilliam.
Fitzwilliam who?
Fitzwilliam better than it fits me.

Knock knock.
Who's there?
Flea.
Flea who?
Flea thirty!

Knock knock.
Who's there?
Flea.
Flea who?
Flea blind mice.

Knock knock.
Who's there?
Fletcher.
Fletcher who?
Fletcher stick, there's a good boy.

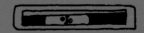

Knock knock.
Who's there?
Fleur.
Fleur who?
Fleuride toothpaste.

Knock knock.
Who's there?
Flo.
Flo who?
Flo your candles out.

Knock knock.
Who's there?
Flora.
Flora who?
Florat the top of the block.

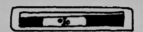

Knock knock.
Who's there?
Florida.
Florida who?
Florida room is sticky.

Knock knock.
Who's there?
Flossie.
Flossie who?
Flossie your teeth every day.

Knock knock.
Who's there?
Flute.
Flute who?
Flute in the basement –
  everything's wet.

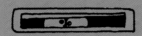

Knock knock.
Who's there?
Fly.
Fly who?
Fly away soon.

Knock knock.
Who's there?
Fonda.
Fonda who?
Fonda my family.

Knock knock.
Who's there?
Foot.
Foot who?
Foot two pence I'd go away now.

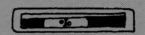

Knock knock.
Who's there?
Fork.
Fork who?
Forket her – she wasn't worth it.

Knock knock.
Who's there?
Forster.
Forster who?
Forstern issue.

Knock knock.
Who's there?
Foster.
Foster who?
Foster than a speeding bullet.

Knock knock.
Who's there?
Francis.
Francis who?
Francis next to Germany.

Knock knock.
Who's there?
Francis.
Francis who?
Francis where the French live.

Knock knock.
Who's there?
Francoise.
Francoise who?
Francoise once a great empire.

Knock knock.
Who's there?
Frank.
Frank who?
Frank you very much.

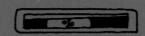

Knock knock.
Who's there?
Franz.
Franz who?
Franz, Romans, countrymen, lend me
    your ears.

Knock knock.
Who's there?
Fred.
Fred who?
Fred I've got some bad news.

Knock knock.
Who's there?
Fred.
Fred who?
Fred this needle – I'm cross-eyed.

Knock knock.
Who's there?
Freddie.
Freddie who?
Freddie won't come out to play
    today.

Knock knock.
Who's there?
Freddie.
Freddie who?
Freddie, steady, go!

Knock knock.
Who's there?
Freddie and Abel.
Freddie and Abel who?
Freddie and Abel to do business.

Knock knock.
Who's there?
Friends.
Friends who?
Friends-ied attack.

Knock knock.
Who's there?
Fruit.
Fruit who?
Fruit of all evil.

Knock knock.
Who's there?
Fudge.
Fudge who?
Fudge up – there's no room!

Knock knock.
Who's there?
Furry.
Furry who?
Furry's a jolly good fellow!

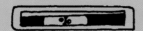

Knock knock.
Who's there?
Gail.
Gail who?
Gail of laughter.

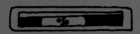

Knock knock.
Who's there?
Galway.
Galway who?
Galway you silly boy.

Knock knock.
Who's there?
Gandhi.
Gandhi who?
Gandhi come out to play?

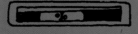

Knock knock.
Who's there?
Gary.
Gary who?
Gary on smiling.

Knock knock.
Who's there?
Gaskill.
Gaskill who?
Gaskills if it's not turned off.

Knock knock.
Who's there?
Gazza.
Gazza who?
Gazza kiss.

Knock knock.
Who's there?
Genoa.
Genoa who?
Genoa good teacher?

Knock knock.
Who's there?
Geoff.
Geoff who?
Geoff feel like going out tonight?

Knock knock.
Who's there?
Gerald.
Gerald who?
Gerald man from round the corner.

Knock knock.
Who's there?
Germaine.
Germaine who?
Germaine you don't recognize me?

Knock knock.
Who's there?
Gertie.
Gertie who?
Gertiesy call.

Knock knock.
Who's there?
Ghana.
Ghana who?
Ghana get me some wheels and hit
    the town!

Knock knock.
Who's there?
Ghent.
Ghent who?
Ghent out of town.

Knock knock.
Who's there?
Ghost.
Ghost who?
Ghost town.

Knock knock.
Who's there?
Ghoul.
Ghoul who?
Ghoulpost painter.

Knock knock.
Who's there?
Gilda.
Gilda who?
Gilda the picture frame.

Knock knock.
Who's there?
Ginny.
Ginny who?
Ginny pig.

Knock knock.
Who's there?
Giovanni.
Giovanni who?
Giovanniny more coffee?

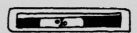

Knock knock.
Who's there?
Giselle.
Giselle who?
Gisellegant and very pretty.

Knock knock.
Who's there?
Gita.
Gita who?
Gita job!

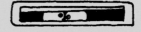

Knock knock.
Who's there?
Giuseppe.
Giuseppe who?
Giuseppe credit cards?

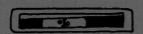

Knock knock.
Who's there?
Gladys.
Gladys who?
Gladys letter isn't a bill.

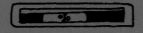

Knock knock.
Who's there?
Glasgow.
Glasgow who?
Glasgow to the theater.

Knock knock.
Who's there?
Goose.
Goose who?
Goose who's knocking at the door!

Knock knock.
Who's there?
Gopher.
Gopher who?
Gopher help – I'm stuck in the mud.

Knock knock.
Who's there?
Gorilla.
Gorilla who?
Gorilla sausage.

Knock knock.
Who's there?
Grace.
Grace who?
Grace your knee.

Knock knock.
Who's there?
Grace.
Grace who?
Grace skies are over us.

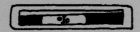

Knock knock.
Who's there?
Grant.
Grant who?
Grant three wishes.

Knock knock.
Who's there?
Grapes.
Grapes who?
Grapes Suzette.

Knock knock.
Who's there?
Gray.
Gray who?
Grayt balls of fire!

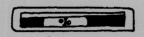

Knock knock.
Who's there?
Greece.
Greece who?
Greece my palm and I'll tell you.

Knock knock.
Who's there?
Greene.
Greene who?
Greene is my valley.

Knock knock.
Who's there?
Greg.
Greg who?
Greg Scott!

Knock knock.
Who's there?
Greta.
Greta who?
Greta job.

Knock knock.
Who's there?
Grimm.
Grimm who?
Grimm and bear it.

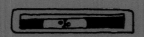

Knock knock.
Who's there?
Grub.
Grub who?
Grub hold of my hand and let's go!

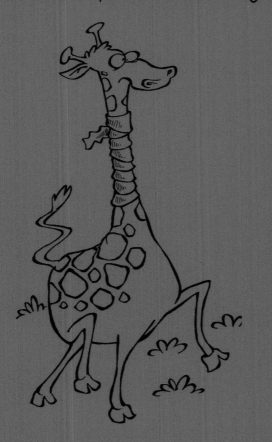

Knock knock.
Who's there?
Guinea.
Guinea who?
Guinea a high five!

Knock knock.
Who's there?
Guinevere.
Guinevere who?
Guinevere going to get together?

Knock knock.
Who's there?
Gus.
Gus who?
Gus what – it's me!

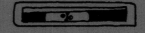

Knock knock.
Who's there?
Guthrie.
Guthrie who?
Guthrie ice creams in my hand.

Knock knock.
Who's there?
Haden.
Haden who?
Haden in the bushes.

Knock knock.
Who's there?
Hair.
Hair who?
Hair you go!

Knock knock.
Who's there?
Haiti.
Haiti who?
Haitit when you talk like that!

Knock knock.
Who's there?
Haiti.
Haiti who?
Haiti-nything to do with witches!

Knock knock.
Who's there?
Hallie.
Hallie who?
Hallie-tosis – your breath smells
    awful!

Knock knock.
Who's there?
Hand.
Hand who?
Handover your money.

Knock knock.
Who's there?
Handel.
Handel who?
Handel with care.

Knock knock.
Who's there?
Hank.
Hank who?
Hank you for asking.

Knock knock.
Who's there?
Hannah.
Hannah who?
Hannah cloth out to dry.

Knock knock.
Who's there?
Hans.
Hans who?
Hans across the sea.

Knock knock.
Who's there?
Harmony.
Harmony who?
Harmony times must I tell you not to
    do that!

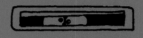

Knock knock.
Who's there?
Hardy.
Hardy who?
Hardy annual.

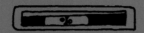

Knock knock.
Who's there?
Harp.
Harp who?
Harp the Herald Angels Sing!

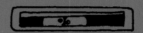

Knock knock.
Who's there?
Harlow.
Harlow who?
Harlow can you get?

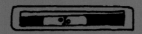

Knock knock.
Who's there?
Harriet.
Harriet who?
Harriet up!

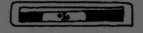

Knock knock.
Who's there?
Harrison.
Harrison who?
Harrison is a credit to his father.

Knock knock.
Who's there?
Harry.
Harry who?
Harry up!

Knock knock.
Who's there?
Havana.
Havana who?
Havana spooky old time!

Knock knock.
Who's there?
Hawaii.
Hawaii who?
Hawaii getting on?

Knock knock.
Who's there?
Hayden.
Hayden who?
Hayden behind the door.

Knock knock.
Who's there?
Hazel.
Hazel who?
Hazel restrict your vision.

Knock knock.
Who's there?
Heather.
Heather who?
Heather pothtman come yet?

Knock knock.
Who's there?
Hedda.
Hedda who?
Hedda ball in goal.

Knock knock.
Who's there?
Heidi.
Heidi who?
Heidi hi campers!

Knock knock.
Who's there?
Heidi.
Heidi who?
Heidi Clare war on you.

Knock knock.
Who's there?
Herman.
Herman who?
Herman dry.

Knock knock.
Who's there?
Herman.
Herman who?
Herman Munster.

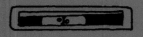

Knock knock.
Who's there?
Hester.
Hester who?
Hester la vista!

Knock knock.
Who's there?
Heywood.
Heywood who?
Heywood you open the door?

Knock knock.
Who's there?
Hip.
Hip who?
Hippopotamus.

Knock knock.
Who's there?
Holly.
Holly who?
Hollylujah!

Knock knock.
Who's there?
Honda.
Honda who?
Honda stand what I'm talking about?

Knock knock.
Who's there?
Hiram.
Hiram who?
Hiram and fire 'em.

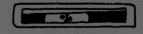

Knock knock.
Who's there?
Hope.
Hope who?
Hope you'll have me.

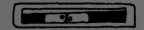

Knock knock.
Who's there?
Hobbit.
Hobbit who?
Hobbit-forming.

Knock knock.
Who's there?
Horatio.
Horatio who?
Horatio to the end of the road.

Knock knock.
Who's there?
Horn.
Horn who?
Horn the way home.

Knock knock.
Who's there?
Hosanna.
Hosanna who?
Hosanna Claus gets down our tiny
    chimney I'll never know!

Knock knock.
Who's there?
House.
House who?
Hugh's fine thanks. How's John?

Knock knock.
Who's there?
Howard.
Howard who?
Howard you know? You won't even
    open up.

Knock knock.
Who's there?
Howard.
Howard who?
Howard you like to stand out here in
the cold while some idiot keeps
saying "Who's there?"

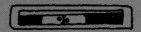

Knock knock.
Who's there?
Howie.
Howie who?
Fine thanks. How are you?

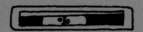

Knock knock.
Who's there?
Howl.
Howl who?
Howl I know when it's supper time?

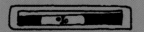

Knock knock.
Who's there?
Huey.
Huey who?
Who am I? I'm me!

Knock knock.
Who's there?
Hugh.
Hugh who?
Hugh wouldn't believe it if I told you.

Knock knock.
Who's there?
Ian.
Ian who?
Ian a lot of money.

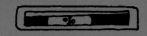

Knock knock.
Who's there?
Ice cream.
Ice cream who?
Ice cream loudly.

Knock knock.
Who's there?
Ida.
Ida who?
Ida thought you could say please.

Knock knock.
Who's there?
Ida.
Ida who?
Ida nawful time at school today.

Knock knock.
Who's there?
Ida.
Ida who?
Ida bought a different knocker if I'd
    been you.

Knock knock.
Who's there?
Ida.
Ida who?
Ida know.

Knock knock.
Who's there?
Ike.
Ike who?
Ike'n see you through the keyhole.

Knock knock.
Who's there?
Imogen.
Imogen who?
Imogenuine person.

Knock knock.
Who's there?
Ina.
Ina who?
Ina minute I'm going to knock the
    door down!

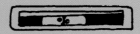

Knock knock.
Who's there?
Ina Claire.
Ina Claire who?
Ina Claire day you can see forever.

Knock knock.
Who's there?
Ina Minnie.
Ina Minnie who?
Ina Minnie miney mo.

Knock knock.
Who's there?
India.
India who?
India there's a bag belonging to me.

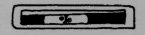

Knock knock.
Who's there?
Ines.
Ines who?
Inespecial place I'll hide your
    present.

Knock knock.
Who's there?
Ingrid.
Ingrid who?
Ingrid sorrow I have to leave you.

Knock knock.
Who's there?
Insect.
Insect who?
Insect your name and address here.

Knock knock.
Who's there?
Iona.
Iona who?
Iona house of my own, you know.

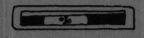

Knock knock.
Who's there?
Iowa.
Iowa who?
Iowa lot to you.

Knock knock.
Who's there?
Ira.
Ira who?
Irate – or I will be if I stand out here
    any longer!

Knock knock.
Who's there?
Iran.
Iran who?
Iran all the way here. Let me in!

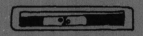

Knock knock.
Who's there?
Iraq.
Iraq who?
Iraq of lamb for dinner, please.

Knock knock.
Who's there?
Isabel.
Isabel who?
Isabel necessary on a bicycle?

Knock knock.
Who's there?
Isabella.
Isabella who?
Isabella dingdong?

Knock knock.
Who's there?
Iris.
Iris who?
Iris you would open the door.

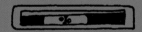

Knock knock.
Who's there?
Isadore.
Isadore who?
Isadore on the right way round?

Knock knock.
Who's there?
Isaac.
Isaac who?
Isaac all my staff today.

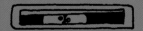

Knock knock.
Who's there?
Isla.
Isla who?
Isla be seeing you.

Knock knock.
Who's there?
Ivan.
Ivan who?
Ivan enormous snake in my pocket.

Knock knock.
Who's there?
Ivan.
Ivan who?
Ivan the history prize.

Knock knock.
Who's there?
Ivana.
Ivana who?
Ivana be alone.

Knock knock.
Who's there?
Ivor.
Ivor who?
Ivor lot more jokes where this came
    from.

Knock knock.
Who's there?
Ivy.
Ivy who?
Ivyll cast a spell on you.

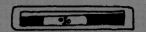

Knock knock.
Who's there?
Jack.
Jack who?
Jack in the box.

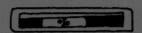

Knock knock.
Who's there?
Jackie.
Jackie who?
Jackie'n that job – it's killing you.

Knock knock.
Who's there?
Jacqueline.
Jacqueline who?
Jacqueline Hyde.

Knock knock.
Who's there?
Jade.
Jade who?
Jade a whole pie today.

Knock knock.
Who's there?
Jagger.
Jagger who?
Jaggered edge.

Knock knock.
Who's there?
Jam.
Jam who?
Jam mind! I'm trying to think out
	here.

Knock knock.
Who's there?
Jamaica.
Jamaica who?
Jamaica mistake again?

Knock knock.
Who's there?
James.
James who?
James people play.

Knock knock.
Who's there?
Jamie.
Jamie who?
Jamie'n you don't recognize my
	voice?

Knock knock.
Who's there?
Jan.
Jan who?
Jan and bread.

Knock knock.
Who's there?
Janet.
Janet who?
Janet a big fish?

Knock knock.
Who's there?
Jasmine.
Jasmine who?
Jasmine like to play in bands.

Knock knock.
Who's there?
Jason.
Jason who?
Jason a rainbow.

Knock knock.
Who's there?
Java.
Java who?
Java cat in your house?

Knock knock.
Who's there?
Jaws.
Jaws who?
Jaws which one you want.

Knock knock.
Who's there?
Jay.
Jay who?
Jay what you mean.

Knock knock.
Who's there?
Jay.
Jay who?
Jaylbird with clanking chains.

Knock knock.
Who's there?
Jean.
Jean who?
Jeanius – you just don't recognize it.

Knock knock.
Who's there?
Jeanette.
Jeanette who?
Jeanette has too many holes in it,
    the fish will escape.

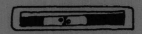

Knock knock.
Who's there?
Jeff.
Jeff who?
Jeff fancy going out tonight?

Knock knock.
Who's there?
Jeffrey.
Jeffrey who?
Jeffrey time I knock, you ask who I
  am.

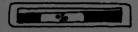

Knock knock.
Who's there?
Jelly Bean.
Jelly Bean who?
Jelly Bean to the sea yet?

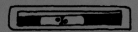

Knock knock.
Who's there?
Jenny.
Jenny who?
Jenny-d anything from the shops?

Knock knock.
Who's there?
Jerome.
Jerome who?
Jerome alone.

Knock knock.
Who's there?
Jerome.
Jerome who?
Jerome alone through the woods
  looking for victims?

Knock knock.
Who's there?
Jerry.
Jerry who?
Jerry cake.

Knock knock.
Who's there?
Jess.
Jess who?
Jess li'l ol' me.

Knock knock.
Who's there?
Jess.
Jess who?
Don't know, you tell me.

Knock knock.
Who's there?
Jesse.
Jesse who?
Jesse if you can recognize my voice.

Knock knock.
Who's there?
Jessica.
Jessica who?
Jessica lot up last night?

Knock knock.
Who's there?
Jester.
Jester who?
Jester silly old man.

Knock knock.
Who's there?
Jethro.
Jethro who?
Jethro our ball back, please?

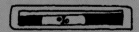

Knock knock.
Who's there?
Jewel.
Jewel who?
Jewel know me when you open the
    door.

Knock knock.
Who's there?
Jez.
Jez who?
Jezt a minute.

Knock knock.
Who's there?
Jim.
Jim who?
Jim mind if we come and stay with
    you?

Knock knock.
Who's there?
Jimmy.
Jimmy who?
Jimmy all your money.

Knock knock.
Who's there?
Joan.
Joan who?
Joan you know your own daughter?

Knock knock.
Who's there?
Joan.
Joan who?
Joan call us, we'll call you.

Knock knock.
Who's there?
Joan.
Joan who?
Joan rush, I'll tell you in a minute.

Knock knock.
Who's there?
Joanna.
Joanna who?
Joanna big kiss?

Knock knock.
Who's there?
Johann.
Johann who?
Johann! How you doing, dude?

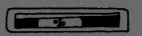

Knock knock.
Who's there?
Joe.
Joe who?
Joe away – I'm not talking to you.

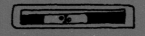

Knock knock.
Who's there?
John.
John who?
John in the fun.

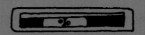

Knock knock.
Who's there?
Joe-jum.
Joe-jum who?
Joe-jum poff a cliff!

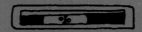

Knock knock.
Who's there?
Joplin.
Joplin who?
Joplin any time you like.

Knock knock.
Who's there?
Julie.
Julie who?
Julie'n on this door a lot?

Knock knock.
Who's there?
Juliet.
Juliet who?
Juliet him get away with that?

Knock knock.
Who's there?
Juliet.
Juliet who?
Juliet so much she burst!

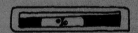

Knock knock.
Who's there?
July.
July who?
July or do you tell the truth?

Knock knock.
Who's there?
June.
June who?
Juneno what time it is?

Knock knock.
Who's there?
June.
June who?
June know how to open a door?

Knock knock.
Who's there?
Juno.
Juno who?
Juno how to get out of here?

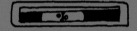

Knock knock.
Who's there?
Jupiter.
Jupiter who?
Jupiter hurry or you'll miss the
    school bus.

Knock knock.
Who's there?
Justin.
Justin who?
Justin time.

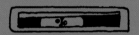

Knock knock.
Who's there?
Justine.
Justine who?
Justine case.

Knock knock.
Who's there?
Karen.
Karen who?
Karen the can for you.

Knock knock.
Who's there?
Katherine.
Katherine who?
Katherine together for a social
  evening.

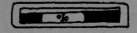

Knock knock.
Who's there?
Kathy.
Kathy who?
Kathy you again?

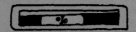

Knock knock.
Who's there?
Keanu.
Keanu who?
Keanu let me in? It's cold out here.

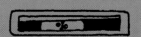

Knock knock.
Who's there?
Keith.
Keith who?
Keith your hands off me!

Knock knock.

Who's there?

Lacey.

Lacey who?

Lacey crazy days.

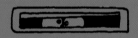

Knock knock.

Who's there?

Lana.

Lana who?

Lana the free.

Knock knock.

Who's there?

Lara.

Lara who?

Lara lara laffs in Liverpool.

Knock knock.

Who's there?

Larry.

Larry who?

Larry up.

Knock knock.

Who's there?

Larva.

Larva who?

Larva cup of coffee.

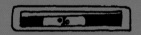

Knock knock.
Who's there?
Laurie.
Laurie who?
Laurie-load of goods.

Knock knock.
Who's there?
Leaf.
Leaf who?
Leaf me be!

Knock knock.
Who's there?
Leah.
Leah who?
Leahn a egg for my breakfast.

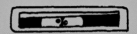

Knock knock.
Who's there?
Lee.
Lee who?
Lee've it to me.

Knock knock.
Who's there?
Len.
Len who?
Len us a fiver will you?

Knock knock.
Who's there?
Leon.
Leon who?
Leon me – I'll support you.

Knock knock.
Who's there?
Leonie.
Leonie who?
Leonie one I love.

Knock knock.
Who's there?
Les.
Les who?
Les see what we can do.

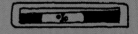

Knock knock.
Who's there?
Leslie.
Leslie who?
Leslie town now before they catch us.

Knock knock.
Who's there?
Lester.
Lester who?
Lester we forget.

Knock knock.
Who's there?
Letter.
Letter who?
Letter in!

Knock knock.
Who's there?
Lettice.
Lettice who?
Lettice in and we'll tell you.

Knock knock.
Who's there?
Lewis.
Lewis who?
Lewis all my money in a poker
    game.

Knock knock.
Who's there?
Lily.
Lily who?
Lily livered varmint.

Knock knock.
Who's there?
Linnekar.
Linnekar who?
Linnekars in a big traffic jam.

Knock knock.
Who's there?
Lisbon.
Lisbon who?
Lisbon away a long time.

Knock knock.
Who's there?
Little old lady.
Little old lady who?
I didn't know you could yodel.

Knock knock.
Who's there?
Lionel.
Lionel who?
Lionel roar if you stand on its tail.

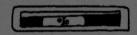

Knock knock.
Who's there?
Liz.
Liz who?
Lizen carefully, I will say this only
    once.

Knock knock.
Who's there?
Lisa.
Lisa who?
Lisa'n life.

Knock knock.
Who's there?
Liz.
Liz who?
Liz see what you look like.

Knock knock.
Who's there?
Lloyd.
Lloyd who?
Lloyd him away with an ice cream.

Knock knock.
Who's there?
Lloyd.
Lloyd who?
Lloydsamoney.

Knock knock.
Who's there?
Lock.
Lock who?
Lock through the peephole.

Knock knock.
Who's there?
Lolly.
Lolly who?
Lollyng about on the sofa.

Knock knock.
Who's there?
Lotte.
Lotte who?
Lotte sense.

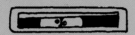

Knock knock.
Who's there?
Lou.
Lou who?
Lou's your money on the horses.

Knock knock.
Who's there?
Louise.
Louise who?
Louise coming to tea today.

Knock knock.
Who's there?
Lucetta.
Lucetta who?
Lucetta a difficult problem.

Knock knock.
Who's there?
Lucille.
Lucille who?
Lucille-ing is dangerous to live
    under.

Knock knock.
Who's there?
Lucinda.
Lucinda who?
(sing) "Lucinda sky with
     diamonds . . ."

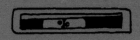

Knock knock.
Who's there?
Lucy.
Lucy who?
Lucylastic can let you down.

Knock knock.
Who's there?
Lulu.
Lulu who?
Lulu's not working, can I use yours?

Knock knock.
Who's there?
Luke.
Luke who?
Luke through the peephole and
     you'll see.

Knock knock.
Who's there?
Lumley.
Lumley who?
Lumley cakes!

Knock knock.
Who's there?
Lyle.
Lyle who?
Lyle low until the cops have gone.

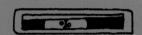

Knock knock.
Who's there?
Luther.
Luther who?
Luther please – not tho tight!

Knock knock.
Who's there?
Madonna.
Madonna who?
Madonna's being mean – tell her
  off!

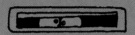

Knock knock.
Who's there?
Madrid.
Madrid who?
Madrid you wash my sports kit?

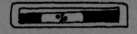

Knock knock.
Who's there?
Mae.
Mae who?
(sing) "Mae be it's because I'm a
  Londoner."

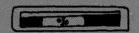

Knock knock.
Who's there?
Maggot.
Maggot who?
Maggot me this new dress today.

Knock knock.
Who's there?
Maia.
Maia who?
Maianimals are like children to me.

Knock knock.
Who's there?
Maine.
Maine who?
Maine reason I'm here!

Knock knock.
Who's there?
Major.
Major who?
Major answer the door didn't I?

Knock knock.
Who's there?
Malcolm.
Malcolm who?
Malcolm outside and play.

Knock knock.
Who's there?
Malt.
Malt who?
Maltesers the girls terribly.

Knock knock.
Who's there?
Mamie.
Mamie who?
Mamie a new dress.

Knock knock.
Who's there?
Mao.
Mao who?
Maothful of toffee.

Knock knock.
Who's there?
March.
March who?
March, march, quick, quick, march.

Knock knock.
Who's there?
Marcia.
Marcia who?
Marcia me!

Knock knock.
Who's there?
Manchu.
Manchu who?
Manchu your food six times.

Knock knock.
Who's there?
Mandy.
Mandy who?
Mandy guns.

Knock knock.
Who's there?
Marcus.
Marcus who?
Marcus a really nice boy.

Knock knock.
Who's there?
Margo.
Margo who?
Margo, you're not needed now.

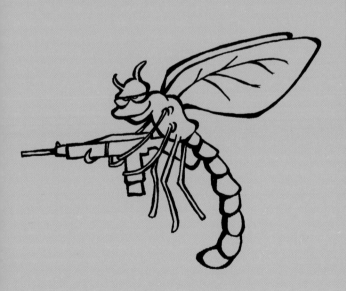

Knock knock.
Who's there?
Maria.
Maria who?
Marial name is Mary.

Knock knock.
Who's there?
Marian.
Marian who?
Mariand her little lamb.

Knock knock.
Who's there?
Marie.
Marie who?
Marie me or I'll cast a spell on you.

Knock knock.
Who's there?
Marie.
Marie who?
Marie for love.

Knock knock.
Who's there?
Marietta.
Marietta who?
Marietta whole loaf!

Knock knock.
Who's there?
Marilyn.
Marilyn who?
Marilyn, she'll make you a good
   wife.

Knock knock.
Who's there?
Marion.
Marion who?
Marion idiot and repent at leisure.

Knock knock.
Who's there?
Mark.
Mark who?
Mark my words.

Knock knock.
Who's there?
Mars.
Mars who?
Marsays you've got to come home
    now.

Knock knock.
Who's there?
Martha.
Martha who?
Martha boys next door are hurting
    me!

Knock knock.
Who's there?
Mary.
Mary who?
That's what I keep wondering.

Knock knock.
Who's there?
Marvin.
Marvin who?
Marvin at these amazing tricks.

Knock knock.
Who's there?
Matthew.
Matthew who?
Matthew lathe hath come undone.

Knock knock.
Who's there?
Maude.
Maude who?
Mauden my job's worth.

Knock knock.
Who's there?
Mauve.
Mauve who?
Mauve over!

Knock knock.
Who's there?
Mavis.
Mavis who?
Mavis be the best day of your life.

Knock knock.
Who's there?
Maude.
Maude who?
Maude of wood.

Knock knock.
Who's there?
Maude.
Maude who?
Mauden living.

Knock knock.
Who's there?
Max.
Max who?
Max Headroom.

Knock knock.
Who's there?
Max.
Max who?
Maximum security is needed in
  these parts.

Knock knock.
Who's there?
Maxine.
Maxine who?
Maxine a lot of things.

Knock knock.
Who's there?
May.
May who?
Maybe it's a friend at the door.

Knock knock.
Who's there?
May.
May who?
May I come in?

Knock knock.
Who's there?
Maya.
Maya who?
Maya turn.

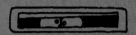

Knock knock.
Who's there?
McEnroe.
McEnroe who?
McEnroe fast with his own oar.

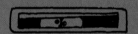

Knock knock.
Who's there?
Me.
Me who?
I didn't know you had a cat!

Knock knock.
Who's there?
Mecca.
Mecca who?
Mecca my day!

Knock knock.
Who's there?
Meg.
Meg who?
Meg a fuss.

162

Knock knock.
Who's there?
Megan.
Megan who?
Megan a cake.

Knock knock.
Who's there?
Megan.
Megan who?
Megan a loud noise.

Knock knock.
Who's there?
Mel.
Mel who?
Melt down!

Knock knock.
Who's there?
Melon.
Melon who?
Melond Kim.

Knock knock.
Who's there?
Metallica.
Metallica who?
Metallicand sleek looks are best for
    cars.

Knock knock.
Who's there?
Michael.
Michael who?
Michaelock has stopped ticking.

Knock knock.
Who's there?
Michael.
Michael who?
Michael beat you up if you don't open the door!

Knock knock.
Who's there?
Michelle.
Michelle who?
Michelle has sounds of the sea in it.

Knock knock.
Who's there?
Mike.
Mike who?
Mike the best of it.

Knock knock.
Who's there?
Mike.
Mike who?
Mike-andle's just blown out. It's all dark.

Knock knock.
Who's there?
Mike and Angelo.
Mike and Angelo who?
Mike and Angelo's David.

Knock knock.
Who's there?
Mikey.
Mikey who?
Mikey is stuck.

Knock knock.
Who's there?
Miles.
Miles who?
Miles away.

Knock knock.
Who's there?
Milo.
Milo who?
Milo bed is too uncomfortable.

Knock knock.
Who's there?
Mimi.
Mimi who?
Mimi b-bicycle's b-broken.

Knock knock.
Who's there?
Minnie.
Minnie who?
Minnie people want to come in.

Knock knock.
Who's there?
Minsk.
Minsk who?
Minsk meat.

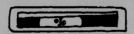

Knock knock.
Who's there?
Mint.
Mint who?
Mint to tell you earlier.

Knock knock.
Who's there?
Miranda.
Miranda who?
Miranda friend want to come in.

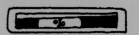

Knock knock.
Who's there?
Misha.
Misha who?
Misha me while I was away?

Knock knock.
Who's there?
Missouri.
Missouri who?
Missouri me! I'm so scared!

Knock knock.
Who's there?
Miss Piggy.
Miss Piggy who?
Miss Piggy went to market, Miss
   Piggy stayed at home . . .

Knock knock.
Who's there?
Money.
Money who?
Money is hurting – I knocked it
   playing football.

Knock knock.
Who's there?
Mom.
Mom who?
Mom's the word.

Knock knock.
Who's there?
Monster.
Monster who?
Monster munch.

Knock knock.
Who's there?
Moses.
Moses who?
Moses the lawn.

Knock knock.
Who's there?
Mosquito.
Mosquito who?
Mosquito smoking soon.

Knock knock.
Who's there?
Moth.
Moth who?
Moth get mythelf a key.

Knock knock.
Who's there?
Morrissey.
Morrissey who?
Morrissey the pretty birdies?

Knock knock.
Who's there?
Moscow.
Moscow who?
Moscow home soon.

Knock knock.
Who's there?
Mountain.
Mountain who?
Mountain debts.

Knock knock.
Who's there?
Mozart.
Mozart who?
Mozart is very beautiful.

Knock knock.
Who's there?
Muffin.
Muffin who?
Muffin to declare.

Knock knock.
Who's there?
Munich.
Munich who?
Munich some money for me?

Knock knock.
Who's there?
Munro.
Munro who?
Munro fast to the other side.

Knock knock.
Who's there?
Murphy.
Murphy who?
Murphy, have murphy! Don't eat me!

Knock knock.
Who's there?
Murphy.
Murphy who?
Murphy, murphy me!

Knock knock.
Who's there?
Murray.
Murray who?
Murray me now.

Knock knock.
Who's there?
Musketeer.
Musketeer who?
Musketeer a doorbell – I'm tired of
    knocking.

Knock knock.
Who's there?
Mustard.
Mustard who?
Mustard left it in the car.

Knock knock.
Who's there?
Myth.
Myth who?
Myth Thmith thilly!

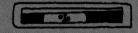

Knock knock.
Who's there?
Nanny.
Nanny who?
Nanny people are waiting to come
   in.

Knock knock.
Who's there?
Nanny.
Nanny who?
Nanny-one home?

Knock knock.
Who's there?
Nadia.
Nadia who?
Nadia head if you want to come in.

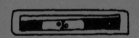

Knock knock.
Who's there?
Neil.
Neil who?
Neil down before the vampire king!

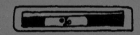

Knock knock.
Who's there?
Nancy.
Nancy who?
Nancy a piece of cake?

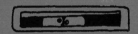

Knock knock.
Who's there?
Nell.
Nell who?
Nell is hot.

Knock knock.
Who's there?
Nestle.
Nestle who?
Nestle into the soft chair.

Knock knock.
Who's there?
Nicholas.
Nicholas who?
Nicholas girls shouldn't climb trees.

Knock knock.
Who's there?
Nick.
Nick who?
Nick R. Elastic.

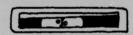

Knock knock.
Who's there?
Nicky.
Nicky who?
Nicky nacks.

Knock knock.
Who's there?
Ninja.
Ninja who?
Ninja with me every day.

Knock knock.
Who's there?
Noah.
Noah who?
Noah counting for taste.

Knock knock.
Who's there?
Noah.
Noah who?
Noah don't know who you are either.

Knock knock.
Who's there?
Nobody.
Nobody who?
Just nobody.

Knock knock.
Who's there?
Noise.
Noise who?
Noise to see you.

Knock knock.
Who's there?
Nola.
Nola who?
Nolaner driver may drive a car
    alone.

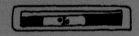

Knock knock.
Who's there?
Norma.
Norma who?
Normally the butler opens the door.

Knock knock.
Who's there?
Norman.
Norman who?
Norman behavior is expected here!

Knock knock.
Who's there?
Norway.
Norway who?
Norway is this your house – it's so
    big!

Knock knock.
Who's there?
Nose.
Nose who?
Nosinging in the house.

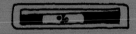

Knock knock.
Who's there?
Nougat.
Nougat who?
Nougat can go that fast!

Knock knock.
Who's there?
Oasis.
Oasis who?
Oasis! Let your brother in!

Knock knock.
Who's there?
Oboe.
Oboe who?
Oboe! I've got the wrong house!

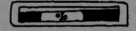

Knock knock.
Who's there?
Oil.
Oil who?
Oil be seeing you.

Knock knock.
Who's there?
Olga.
Olga who?
Olga home now.

Knock knock.
Who's there?
Olga.
Olga who?
Olga way, I can't stand you!

Knock knock.
Who's there?
Olive.
Olive who?
Olive to regret.

Knock knock.

Who's there?

Olive.

Olive who?

Olive in this house – what are you
   doing here?

Knock knock.

Who's there?

Oliver.

Oliver who?

Oliver lone and I'm frightened of
   monsters.

Knock knock.

Who's there?

Oliver.

Oliver who?

Oliver long way away.

Knock knock.

Who's there?

Olivia.

Olivia who?

Olivia'l is great for cooking.

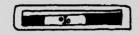

Knock knock.

Who's there?

Olivier.

Olivier who?

Olivier all my money in my will.

Knock knock.
Who's there?
Omar.
Omar who?
Omar goodness, what are you doing
    in there?

Knock knock.
Who's there?
Omelette.
Omelette who?
Omelette smarter than I look!

Knock knock.
Who's there?
One-eye.
One-eye who?
You're the One-eye can't stand!

Knock knock.
Who's there?
Onya.
Onya who?
Onya marks, get set, go.

Knock knock.
Who's there?
Ooze.
Ooze who?
Ooze that knocking at my door?

Knock knock.
Who's there?
Opi.
Opi who?
Opi cushion.

Knock knock.
Who's there?
Orange.
Orange who?
Orange your day to suit the
  weather.

Knock knock.
Who's there?
Organ.
Organ who?
Organize a party – it's my birthday.

Knock knock.
Who's there?
Orson.
Orson who?
Orson, let your daddy in.

Knock knock.
Who's there?
Oscar.
Oscar who?
Oscar foolish question, get a foolish
  answer.

Knock knock.
Who's there?
Othello.
Othello who?
Othello I wouldn't trust an inch.

Knock knock.
Who's there?
Owen.
Owen who?
Owen up, we all know you did it.

Knock knock.
Who's there?
Owl.
Owl who?
Owl I can say is knock knock.

Knock knock.
Who's there?
Owl.
Owl who?
Owl be sad if you don't let me in.

Knock knock.
Who's there?
Owl.
Owl who?
Owl aboard!

Knock knock.
Who's there?
Oz.
Oz who?
Oz got something for you.

Knock knock.
Who's there?
Pablo.
Pablo who?
Pablo the candles out.

Knock knock.
Who's there?
Pam.
Pam who?
Pamper yourself.

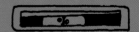

Knock knock.
Who's there?
Pammy.
Pammy who?
Pammy something nice when you
     are at the shops!

Knock knock.
Who's there?
Panon.
Panon who?
Panon my intrusion.

Knock knock.
Who's there?
Panther.
Panther who?
Panther what you wear on your
     legth.

Knock knock.
Who's there?
Paris.
Paris who?
Paris by the vampire very quietly.

Knock knock.
Who's there?
Paris.
Paris who?
Paris the pepper, please.

Knock knock.
Who's there?
Parrot.
Parrot who?
Parrotly you live here.

Knock knock.
Who's there?
Parsley.
Parsley who?
Parsley jam please.

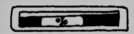

Knock knock.
Who's there?
Parton.
Parton who?
Parton my intrusion.

Knock knock.
Who's there?
Pasta.
Pasta who?
Pasta salt please.

Knock knock.
Who's there?
Pastille.
Pastille who?
Pastille long road you'll find a
    village.

Knock knock.
Who's there?
Patrick.
Patrick who?
Patricked me into coming.

Knock knock.
Who's there?
Patty.
Patty who?
Patty-cake.

Knock knock.
Who's there?
Paul.
Paul who?
Paul up a chair and I'll tell you.

Knock knock.
Who's there?
Paul.
Paul who?
Paul your weight!

Knock knock.
Who's there?
Paul and Portia
Paul and Portia who?
Paul and Portia door to open it.

Knock knock.
Who's there?
Pear.
Pear who?
Pear of shoes.

Knock knock.
Who's there?
Peas.
Peas who?
Peas to meet you.

Knock knock.
Who's there?
Pecan.
Pecan who?
Pecan boo!

Knock knock.
Who's there?
Pecan.
Pecan who?
Pecan work it out.

Knock knock.
Who's there?
Pecan.
Pecan who?
Pecan somebody your own size.

Knock knock.
Who's there?
Peg.
Peg who?
Peg your pardon, I've got the wrong
    door.

Knock knock.
Who's there?
Pen.
Pen who?
Pent-up emotions!

Knock knock.
Who's there?
Pencil.
Pencil who?
Pencil fall down if your belt snaps.

Knock knock.
Who's there?
Penny.
Penny who?
Penny for your thoughts.

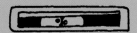

Knock knock.
Who's there?
Pepsi.
Pepsi who?
Pepsi through the peephole.

Knock knock.
Who's there?
Percy.
Percy who?
Percy Verence is the secret of
    success.

Knock knock.
Who's there?
Perry.
Perry who?
Perry well, thank you.

Knock knock.
Who's there?
Perth.
Perth who?
Perth full of money.

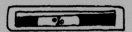

Knock knock.
Who's there?
Peru.
Peru who?
Peruse this map before you go.

Knock knock.
Who's there?
Petal.
Petal who?
Petal fast, we're nearly there.

Knock knock.
Who's there?
Peter.
Peter who?
Peter cake.

Knock knock.
Who's there?
Pfeiffer.
Pfeiffer who?
Pfeiffer hours to Australia.

Knock knock.
Who's there?
Philip.
Philip who?
Philip the car with gas.

Knock knock.
Who's there?
Philippa.
Philippa who?
Philippa a bath – I'm really dirty.

Knock knock.
Who's there?
Phoebe.
Phoebe who?
Phoebe way above my price.

Knock knock.
Who's there?
Piano.
Piano who?
Piano Ferries.

Knock knock.
Who's there?
Pickle.
Pickle who?
That's my favorite instrument.

Knock knock.
Who's there?
Phone.
Phone who?
Phone I'd known it was you.

Knock knock.
Who's there?
Pierre.
Pierre who?
Pierre through the keyhole – you'll
    see.

Knock knock.
Who's there?
Phyllis.
Phyllis who?
Phyllis up.

Knock knock.
Who's there?
Pill.
Pill who?
Pill you open the door?

Knock knock.
Who's there?
Pizza.
Pizza who?
Pizza this, piece of that.

Knock knock.
Who's there?
Pizza.
Pizza who?
Pizza the action.

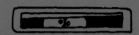

Knock knock.
Who's there?
Plato.
Plato who?
Plato bacon and eggs, please.

Knock knock.
Who's there?
Plums.
Plums who?
Plums me you won't tell.

Knock knock.
Who's there?
Police.
Police who?
Police open the door.

Knock knock.
Who's there?
Polly.
Polly who?
Polly the other one, it's got bells on.

Knock knock.
Who's there?
Poppy.
Poppy who?
Poppy'n any time you like.

Knock knock.
Who's there?
Portia.
Portia who?
Portia the door – it's stuck.

Knock knock.
Who's there?
Posie.
Posie who?
Posie hard questions.

Knock knock.
Who's there?
Pudding.
Pudding who?
Pudding our best feet forward.

Knock knock.
Who's there?
Pulp.
Pulp who?
Pulp pretty hard on the door – it's
   stiff.

Knock knock.
Who's there?
Punch.
Punch who?
Punch you on the nose if you don't
   shut up!

Knock knock.
Who's there?
Puss.
Puss who?
Puss the door – it won't open.

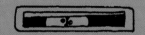

Knock knock.
Who's there?
Python.
Python who?
Python with your pocket money.

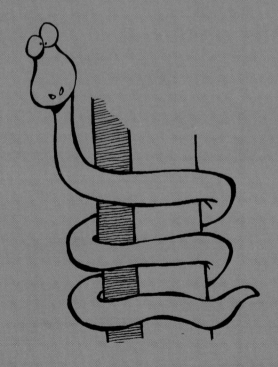

Knock knock.
Who's there?
Quebec.
Quebec who?
Quebec there, if you want a ticket.

Knock knock.
Who's there?
Queen.
Queen who?
Queen of the crop.

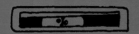

Knock knock.
Who's there?
Quiet Tina.
Quiet Tina who?
Quiet Tina classroom.

Knock knock.
Who's there?
Radio.
Radio who?
Radio not, it's time for school.

Knock knock.
Who's there?
Ralph.
Ralph who?
Ralph, ralph – I'm just a puppy.

Knock knock.
Who's there?
Raoul.
Raoul who?
Raoul of law.

Knock knock.
Who's there?
Rattlesnake.
Rattlesnake who?
Rattlesnake a big difference!

Knock knock.
Who's there?
Ray.
Ray who?
Ray drops keep falling on my head.

Knock knock.
Who's there?
Ray.
Ray who?
Rayning cats and dogs.

Knock knock.
Who's there?
Raymond.
Raymond who?
Raymond me to take that book
    back.

Knock knock.
Who's there?
Razor.
Razor who?
Razor laugh at that joke.

Knock knock.
Who's there?
Recorder.
Recorder who?
Recorder film for me tonight, will
    you?

Knock knock.
Who's there?
Red.
Red who?
Red any good books lately?

Knock knock.
Who's there?
Rena.
Rena who?
Renamok in the shopping mall.

Knock knock.
Who's there?
Renata.
Renata who?
Renata sugar. Can I borrow some?

Knock knock.
Who's there?
Reuben.
Reuben who?
Reuben my eyes.

Knock knock.
Who's there?
Rhona.
Rhona who?
Rhonaround town.

Knock knock.
Who's there?
Rhonda.
Rhonda who?
Rhonda why?

Knock knock.
Who's there?
Richard.
Richard who?
Richard poor have little in common.

Knock knock.
Who's there?
Ringo.
Ringo who?
Ringof truth.

Knock knock.
Who's there?
Rio.
Rio who?
Riorrange your appointment please.

Knock knock.
Who's there?
Rita.
Rita who?
Rita novel.

Knock knock.
Who's there?
Roach.
Roach who?
Roach out and touch somebody.

Knock knock.
Who's there?
Robert.
Robert who?
Roberts are taking over the world.

Knock knock.
Who's there?
Robin.
Robin who?
Robin banks.

Knock knock.
Who's there?
Roland.
Roland who?
Roland stone gathers no moss.

Knock knock.
Who's there?
Roland.
Roland who?
Roland butter please.

Knock knock.
Who's there?
Rome.
Rome who?
Roming around.

Knock knock.
Who's there?
Romeo.
Romeo who?
Romeover the river.

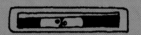

Knock knock.
Who's there?
Ron.
Ron who?
Ron answer.

Knock knock.
Who's there?
Ron.
Ron who?
Ron way round.

Knock knock.
Who's there?
Rose.
Rose who?
Rose early one morning.

Knock knock.
Who's there?
Rosie.
Rosie who?
Rosie-lee is the best cuppa in the
    morning.

Knock knock.
Who's there?
Rosina.
Rosina who?
Rosina vase.

Knock knock.
Who's there?
Rothschild.
Rothschild who?
Rothschild is very clever.

Knock knock.
Who's there?
Roxie.
Roxie who?
Roxie Horror Show.

Knock knock.
Who's there?
Royal.
Royal who?
Royal show you his paintings if you
    ask nicely.

Knock knock.
Who's there?
R.U.
R.U. who?
R.U. really as stupid as you seem?

Knock knock.
Who's there?
Rudi.
Rudi who?
Rudi toot!

Knock knock.
Who's there?
Russell.
Russell who?
Russelling leaves.

Knock knock.
Who's there?
Russia.
Russia who?
Russia down the shops before they
    close.

Knock knock.
Who's there?
Ruth.
Ruth who?
Ruthless people.

Knock knock.
Who's there?
Ryder.
Ryder who?
Ryder fast horse.

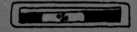

Knock knock.
Who's there?
Sacha.
Sacha who?
Sacha money in the bank.

Knock knock.
Who's there?
Sacha.
Sacha who?
Sacha lot of questions in this exam.

Knock knock.
Who's there?
Saddam.
Saddam who?
Saddam I that you couldn't come to
    the party.

Knock knock.
Who's there?
Saffron.
Saffron who?
Saffron a chair and it collapsed.

Knock knock.
Who's there?
Sally.
Sally who?
Sallyeverything you've got.

Knock knock.
Who's there?
Sam.
Sam who?
Sam day you'll recognize my voice.

Knock knock.
Who's there?
Samantha.
Samantha who?
Samantha baby have gone for a
   walk.

Knock knock.
Who's there?
Sandra.
Sandra who?
Sandrabout your toes on the beach.

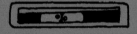

Knock knock.
Who's there?
Sandy.
Sandy who?
Sandy shore.

Knock knock.
Who's there?
Sarah.
Sarah who?
Sarah doctor in the house?

Knock knock.
Who's there?
Saul.
Saul who?
Saul I know.

Knock knock.
Who's there?
Scargill.
Scargill who?
Scargill not go any faster.

Knock knock.
Who's there?
Scissor.
Scissor who?
Scissor was a Roman emperor.

Knock knock.
Who's there?
Scold.
Scold who?
Scold outside. Please let me in.

Knock knock.
Who's there?
Scott.
Scott who?
Scott land the brave.

Knock knock.
Who's there?
Scott.
Scott who?
Scott nothing to do with you.

Knock knock.
Who's there?
Scott.
Scott who?
Scott a nasty look about it, has this place. Is it haunted?

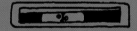

Knock knock.
Who's there?
Scully.
Scully who?
Scully-wag!

Knock knock.
Who's there?
Sebastian.
Sebastian who?
Sebastian of society.

Knock knock.
Who's there?
Serena.
Serena who?
Serena round the corner.

Knock knock.
Who's there?
Serena.
Serena who?
Serena round Saturn.

Knock knock.
Who's there?
Serpent.
Serpent who?
Serpents are working hard, sir.

Knock knock.
Who's there?
Seville.
Seville who?
Seville Row suit.

Knock knock.
Who's there?
Seymour.
Seymour who?
Seymour from the top window.

Knock knock.
Who's there?
Sharon.
Sharon who?
Sharon share alike.

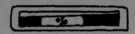

Knock knock.
Who's there?
Sheik and Geisha.
Sheik and Geisha who?
Sheik and Geisha'll find.

Knock knock.
Who's there?
Shelby.
Shelby who?
(sing) "Shelby coming round the mountain when she comes."

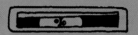

Knock knock.
Who's there?
Sherlock.
Sherlock who?
Sherlock your door – someone could break in.

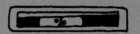

Knock knock.
Who's there?
Sherry.
Sherry who?
Sherry trifle!

Knock knock.
Who's there?
Sheryl Crow.
Sheryl Crow who?
Sheryl Crow to the movies tonight?

Knock knock.
Who's there?
Shields.
Shields who?
Shields say anything.

Knock knock.
Who's there?
Shirley.
Shirley who?
Shirley you know who I am?

Knock knock.
Who's there?
Shoes.
Shoes who?
Shoes me, I didn't mean to stand on your foot.

Knock knock.
Who's there?
Sid.
Sid who?
Sid on it!

Knock knock.
Who's there?
Sienna.
Sienna who?
Siennathing good at the movies?

Knock knock.
Who's there?
Sigrid.
Sigrid who?
Sigrid Service.

Knock knock.
Who's there?
Simon.
Simon who?
Simon time again I've told you not to
   do that.

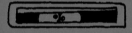

Knock knock.
Who's there?
Sis.
Sis who?
Sisteen Chapel.

Knock knock.
Who's there?
Sloane.
Sloane who?
Sloanely outside – let me in.

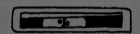

Knock knock.
Who's there?
Smarties.
Smarties who?
Smartiest kid in the class.

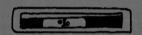

Knock knock.
Who's there?
Smee.
Smee who?
Smee, your friend.

Knock knock.
Who's there?
Snake.
Snake who?
Snake a run for it.

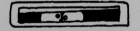

Knock knock.
Who's there?
Snickers.
Snickers who?
Snickers at me because I'm small.

Knock knock.
Who's there?
Snow.
Snow who?
Snow business of yours.

Knock knock.
Who's there?
Sondheim.
Sondheim who?
Sondheim soon we'll meet again.

Knock knock.
Who's there?
Sonia.
Sonia who?
Sonia shoe – it's stinking the house out!

Knock knock.
Who's there?
Sonia.
Sonia who?
Sonia me!

Knock knock.
Who's there?
Sonny.
Sonny who?
Sonny outside, isn't it?

Knock knock.
Who's there?
Sophia.
Sophia who?
Sophia nothing . . . fear is pointless.

Knock knock.
Who's there?
Sorrel.
Sorrel who?
Sorrel about the mess.

Knock knock.
Who's there?
Soup.
Soup who?
Souper Mom!

Knock knock.
Who's there?
Spain.
Spain who?
Spaint all over the wall!

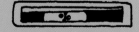

Knock knock.
Who's there?
Spell.
Spell who?
Spelling test.

Knock knock.
Who's there?
Spice.
Spice who?
Spice satellites are orbiting the
    earth.

Knock knock.
Who's there?
Spider.
Spider who?
Spider through the keyhole.

Knock knock.
Who's there?
Spider.
Spider who?
Spider when she thought I wasn't
    looking.

Knock knock.
Who's there?
Spock.
Spock who?
Spocken like a true gentleman.

Knock knock.
Who's there?
Stacey.
Stacey who?
Stacey what happens next.

Knock knock.
Who's there?
Stalin.
Stalin who?
Stalin for time.

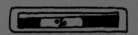

Knock knock.
Who's there?
Stan.
Stan who?
Stan back, I'm going to be sick.

Knock knock.
Who's there?
Stan and Della.
Stan and Della who?
Stan and Dellaver.

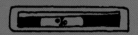

Knock knock.
Who's there?
Stefan.
Stefan who?
Stefan it!

Knock knock.
Who's there?
Stella.
Stella who?
Stella lot from the rich people.

Knock knock.
Who's there?
Stephanie.
Stephanie who?
Stephanie gas – we need to go
   faster!

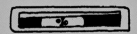

Knock knock.
Who's there?
Steve.
Steve who?
Steve upper lip.

Knock knock.
Who's there?
Stevie.
Stevie who?
Stevie has terrible reception.

Knock knock.
Who's there?
Stones.
Stones who?
Stones sober.

Knock knock.
Who's there?
Stopwatch.
Stopwatch who?
Stopwatch you're doing this minute!

Knock knock.
Who's there?
Street.
Street who?
Street to go out to dinner.

Knock knock.
Who's there?
Stu.
Stu who?
Stu late to go to school now.

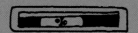

Knock knock.
Who's there?
Sue.
Sue who?
Sue'n you will know.

Knock knock.
Who's there?
Summer.
Summer who?
Summer good, some are bad.

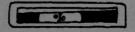

Knock knock.
Who's there?
Supergrass.
Supergrass who?
Supergrass on your lawn!

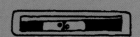

Knock knock.
Who's there?
Sweden.
Sweden who?
Sweden the pill.

Knock knock.
Who's there?
Sybil.
Sybil who?
Sybiling rivalry.

Knock knock.
Who's there?
Tamsin.
Tamsin who?
Tamsin time again I come to the
    wrong house.

Knock knock.
Who's there?
Talbot.
Talbot who?
Talbot too thin.

Knock knock.
Who's there?
Tango.
Tango who?
Tango faster than this you know.

Knock knock.
Who's there?
Tamara.
Tamara who?
Tamara's the day of the school
    concert.

Knock knock.
Who's there?
Tania.
Tania who?
Tania self round, you'll see.

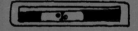

Knock knock.
Who's there?
Tara.
Tara who?
Tararaboomdeay.

Knock knock.
Who's there?
Tariq.
Tariq who?
Tariq of perfume will put anyone off.

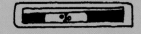

Knock knock.
Who's there?
Tarzan.
Tarzan who?
Tarzan stripes forever!

Knock knock.
Who's there?
Teacher.
Teacher who?
Teacher-self French.

Knock knock.
Who's there?
Teacher.
Teacher who?
Teacher to copy my answers!

Knock knock.
Who's there?
Teheran.
Teheran who?
Teheran and look me in the eye.

Knock knock.
Who's there?
Teheran.
Teheran who?
Teheran very slowly – there's a
    monster behind you.

Knock knock.
Who's there?
Telly.
Telly who?
Telly your friend to come out.

Knock knock.
Who's there?
Tennis.
Tennis who?
Tennis five plus five.

Knock knock.
Who's there?
Tennis.
Tennis who?
Tennis two times five.

Knock knock.
Who's there?
Termite.
Termite who?
Termite's the night!

Knock knock.
Who's there?
Thatcher.
Thatcher who?
Thatcher car? Rubbish, innit!

Knock knock.
Who's there?
Thea.
Thea who?
Thea later alligator.

Knock knock.
Who's there?
Thea.
Thea who?
Thea ghost?

Knock knock.
Who's there?
Theodore.
Theodore who?
Theodore is locked.

Knock knock.
Who's there?
Thighs.
Thighs who?
Thighs the limit.

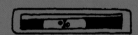

Knock knock.
Who's there?
Thistle.
Thistle who?
Thistle be the last time I knock.

Knock knock.
Who's there?
Theresa.
Theresa who?
Theresa green.

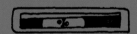

Knock knock.
Who's there?
Thomas.
Thomas who?
Thomaster a language takes a long
    time.

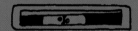

Knock knock.
Who's there?
Thermos.
Thermos who?
Thermos be a better player than
    you.

Knock knock.
Who's there?
Throat.
Throat who?
Throat to me.

Knock knock.
Who's there?
Thumb.
Thumb who?
Thumb like it hot.

Knock knock.
Who's there?
Thumping.
Thumping who?
Thumping green and slimy is
     creeping up your leg.

Knock knock.
Who's there?
Thumping.
Thumping who?
Thumping's jutht knocked my teef
     out.

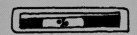

Knock knock.
Who's there?
Tic tac.
Tic tac who?
Tic tac paddy whack, give the dog a
     bone.

Knock knock.
Who's there?
Tick.
Tick who?
Tick 'em up and gimme all your
   money.

Knock knock.
Who's there?
Tiffany.
Tiffany who?
Tiffany rubbish out of the bag
   before you use it.

Knock knock.
Who's there?
Tilly.
Tilly who?
Tilly learns to say please, he'll stay
   outside.

Knock knock.
Who's there?
Tilly.
Tilly who?
Tilly cows come home.

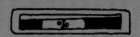

Knock knock.
Who's there?
Tim.
Tim who?
Tim after time.

Knock knock.
Who's there?
Tim.
Tim who?
Tim you got scared.

Knock knock.
Who's there?
Tina.
Tina who?
Tina tomatoes.

Knock knock.
Who's there?
Toby.
Toby who?
Toby or not Toby, that is the
     question.

Knock knock.
Who's there?
Toffee.
Toffee who?
Toffeel loved is the best feeling in
     the world.

Knock knock.
Who's there?
Tommy.
Tommy who?
Tommy you will always be beautiful.

Knock knock.
Who's there?
Tom Sawyer.
Tom Sawyer who?
Tom Sawyer bum when you were
     changing your trousers.

Knock knock.
Who's there?
Tooth.
Tooth who?
Tooth or dare.

Knock knock.
Who's there?
Too whit.
Too whit who?
Is there an owl in the house?

Knock knock.
Who's there?
Topic.
Topic who?
Topic a wild flower is against the law.

Knock knock.
Who's there?
Tori.
Tori who?
Tori I upset you.

Knock knock.
Who's there?
Toto.
Toto who?
Totolly devoted to you.

Knock knock.
Who's there?
Toyota.
Toyota who?
Toyota be a law against people like
  you.

Knock knock.
Who's there?
Tracy.
Tracy who?
Tracy the shape in pencil.

Knock knock.
Who's there?
Tricia.
Tricia who?
Bless you – what a bad cold!

Knock knock.
Who's there?
Tristan.
Tristan who?
Tristan insect to really get up your
  nose.

Knock knock.
Who's there?
Tristan.
Tristan who?
Tristan elephant not to forget.

Knock knock.
Who's there?
Troy.
Troy who?
Troy the bell instead.

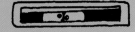

Knock knock.
Who's there?
Trudy.
Trudy who?
Trudy your word.

Knock knock.
Who's there?
Truffle.
Truffle who?
Truffle with you is you are so shy.

Knock knock.
Who's there?
Truman.
Truman who?
Truman and good needed for the
    jury.

Knock knock.
Who's there?
Trump.
Trump who?
Trumped-up charges.

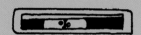

Knock knock.
Who's there?
Tubby.
Tubby who?
Tubby or not to be.

Knock knock.
Who's there?
Tummy.
Tummy who?
Tummy you'll always be the best.

Knock knock.
Who's there?
Tuna.
Tuna who?
Tuna whole orchestra.

Knock knock.
Who's there?
Turin.
Turin who?
Turin to a werewolf under a full
   moon.

Knock knock.
Who's there?
Turkey.
Turkey who?
Turkey then you can open the door.

Knock knock.
Who's there?
Turner.
Turner who?
Turner round, there's a monster
   breathing down your neck.

Knock knock.
Who's there?
Turnip.
Turnip who?
Turnip for work at nine or you're
   fired!

Knock knock.
Who's there?
Twix.
Twix who?
Twixt you and me there's a lot of
love.

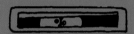

Knock knock.
Who's there?
Twyla.
Twyla who?
Twyla of your life.

Knock knock.
Who's there?
Twyla.
Twyla who?
Twyla is when the ghosties and
ghoulies come out to play!

Knock knock.
Who's there?
Tyson.
Tyson who?
Tyson of this for size.

Knock knock.
Who's there?
UB40.
UB40 who?
UB40 today – happy birthday!

Knock knock.
Who's there?
Uganda.
Uganda who?
Uganda go away now.

Knock knock.
Who's there?
Una.
Una who?
Yes, Una who.

Knock knock.
Who's there?
Underwear.
Underwear who?
Underwear my baby is tonight?

Knock knock.
Who's there?
Uttica.
Uttica who?
(sing) "Uttica high road and I'll take the low road."

UNIVERSE
THIS
WAY

Knock knock.
Who's there?
Vampire.
Vampire who?
Vampire state building.

Knock knock.
Who's there?
Vanda.
Vanda who?
Vanda you vant me to come round?

Knock knock.
Who's there?
Vanessa.
Vanessa who?
Vanessa time I'll ring the bell.

Knock knock.
Who's there?
Vault.
Vault who?
Vaultsing Matilda.

Knock knock.
Who's there?
Venice.
Venice who?
Venice this going to end?

Knock knock.
Who's there?
Verdi.
Verdi who?
Verdia want to go?

Knock knock.
Who's there?
Vic.
Vic who?
Victim of a vampire.

Knock knock.
Who's there?
Vic.
Vic who?
Victory parade.

Knock knock.
Who's there?
Victor.
Victor who?
Victor his football shorts.

Knock knock.
Who's there?
Vincent.
Vincent who?
Vincent alive anymore.

Knock knock.
Who's there?
Vincent.
Vincent who?
Vincent me here.

Knock knock.
Who's there?
Viola.
Viola who?
Viola sudden you don't know who I am?

Knock knock.
Who's there?
Violet.
Violet who?
Violet the cat out of the bag.

Knock knock.
Who's there?
Violin.
Violin who?
Violin horrible boy.

Knock knock.
Who's there?
Viper.
Viper who?
Viper your nose!

Knock knock.
Who's there?
Visa.
Visa who?
Visa the ones you want.

Knock knock.
Who's there?
Voodoo.
Voodoo who?
Voodoo you think you are?

Knock knock.
Who's there?
Wade.
Wade who?
Wading room.

Knock knock.
Who's there?
Walter.
Walter who?
Walter, walter everywhere and not a
    drop to drink.

Knock knock.
Who's there?
Walter.
Walter who?
Walter wall.

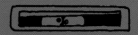

Knock knock.
Who's there?
Ward.
Ward who?
Ward you want?

Knock knock.
Who's there?
Watson.
Watson who?
Watson your head, it looks
    disgusting!

Knock knock.
Who's there?
Watson.
Watson who?
Watson the menu today?

Knock knock.
Who's there?
Wayne.
Wayne who?
(sing) "Wayne in a manger, no crib
   for a bed."

Knock knock.
Who's there?
Webster.
Webster who?
Webster Spin, your friendly
   neighborhood spider.

Knock knock.
Who's there?
Wedgewood.
Wedgewood who?
Wedgewood come if he could but
   he's busy.

Knock knock.
Who's there?
Weevil.
Weevil who?
Weevil work it out.

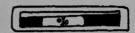

Knock knock.
Who's there?
Weevil.
Weevil who?
Weevil make you talk.

Knock knock.
Who's there?
Wendy.
Wendy who?
Wendy come to take you away I won't stop them!

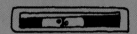

Knock knock.
Who's there?
Wendy.
Wendy who?
Wendy weather we're having.

Knock knock.
Who's there?
Wesley.
Wesley who?
Wesley wind is blowing out here.

Knock knock.
Who's there?
Wet Wet Wet.
Wet Wet Wet who?
Wet Wet Wet out here – pass me an umbrella.

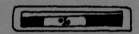

Knock knock.
Who's there?
White.
White who?
White in the middle of it.

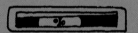

Knock knock.
Who's there?
Whitney.
Whitney who?
Whitneyssed the crime.

Knock knock.
Who's there?
Whoopi.
Whoopi who?
Whoopi cushion.

Knock knock.
Who's there?
Wicked.
Wicked who?
Wicked make beautiful music
    together.

Knock knock.
Who's there?
Wilde.
Wilde who?
Wilde at heart.

Knock knock.
Who's there?
Wilfred.
Wilfred who?
Wilfred come if we ask nicely?

Knock knock.
Who's there?
Will.
Will who?
Will you go away?

Knock knock.
Who's there?
Willa.
Willa who?
Willa present make you happy?

Knock knock.
Who's there?
Wine.
Wine who?
Wine, now you are all grown up!

Knock knock.
Who's there?
Winnie.
Winne who?
Winnie is better than losing.

Knock knock.
Who's there?
Witch.
Witch who?
Witch witch would you like it to be?

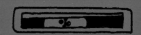

Knock knock.
Who's there?
Wizard.
Wizard who?
Wizard you I'm lost.

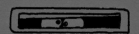

Knock knock.
Who's there?
Wooden shoe.
Wooden shoe who?
Wooden shoe like to know?

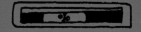

Knock knock.
Who's there?
Woodworm.
Woodworm who?
Woodworm cake be enough or would
   you like two?

Knock knock.
Who's there?
Woody.
Woody who?
Woody come if we asked him?

Knock knock.
Who's there?
Woolf.
Woolf who?
Woolf in sheep's clothing.

Knock knock.
Who's there?
Worm.
Worm who?
Worm in here isn't it?

Knock knock.
Who's there?
Wyn.
Wyn who?
Wyn or lose, it's the taking part that
   counts.

Knock knock.
Who's there?
Wynona.
Wynona who?
Wynona short race.

Knock knock.
Who's there?
Yellow.
Yellow who?
Yellowver the din – I can't hear you.

Knock knock.
Who's there?
Xavier.
Xavier who?
Xavier breath! I'm not leaving.

Knock knock.
Who's there?
Yoga.
Yoga who?
Yoga what it takes!

Knock knock.
Who's there?
Xena.
Xena who?
Xena minute!

Knock knock.
Who's there?
York.
York who?
York, york, york. This is funny.

Knock knock.
Who's there?
You.
You who?
Who's that calling out?

Knock knock.
Who's there?
Yul.
Yul who?
Yuletide.

Knock knock.
Who's there?
Yvette.
Yvette who?
Yvette helps lots of animals.

Knock knock.
Who's there?
Yvonne.
Yvonne who?
Yvonne to know vat you are doing.

Knock knock.
Who's there?
Zippy.
Zippy who?
Zippydidooda, zippydeeay!

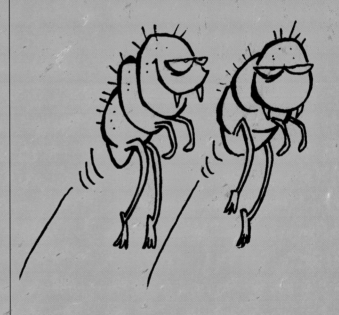

Knock knock.
Who's there?
Zoe.
Zoe who?
Zoe said that, did he? Don't believe
    him.